CÉLINE AUDEBEAU

Dad, you are so beautiful!

NOTES

I HAVE NO LITERARY KNOWLEDGE AND SKILL, I'm very far from considering myself a writer, I just wanted to put my extraordinary adventure on paper. I have the audacity to believe that it can help other people in the same situation, parents, relatives, friends, to give them a new vision of how dysphoric people like to live.

However, I do not consider myself representative of what is called the transgender community. From experience, the worst remarks will come from people also gender dysphoric considering some of my remarks as transphobic.

I accept what I write and never mind comments from sad people, my goal is to give more visibility to transgender people until it becomes a non-topic of discussion or debate. I wish to show a normality, that a very beautiful life is possible after having changed sex.

I am, of course, open to dialogue and criticism as long as it is constructive!

Good reading

Céline Audebeau

Dad, you're so beautiful

INTRODUCTION

Name, first name: Audebeau Christophe

Age: 53 years

Gender: male

Special sign: wants to become a woman

HARD TO PACK THIS BAG, these gestures, I repeated them dozens of times without really paying attention, this time, it is very different. This flight, if everything goes as planned, will be the last one as a man.

Bangkok will become Celine's birthplace. At almost 53 years old, I waited for this moment during ... 48 years. Yet, just three months ago, I wasn't planning any surgery, so much has happened in this short period.

The contents of my suitcase come down to some clothes and some food. Whether in Hanoi, my place of residence, or in Bangkok, the temperature at this time of the year is almost always greater than 35°. Light, light, T-shirts, silk shorts and little dresses.

I want to be a woman but no one has ever seen me "as a woman" except my wife who has been living with me for more than 20 years. My female wardrobe is impressive, years of shopping in catalogs and websites, impossible to go into stores to try products.

All these clothes, stored in my huge closet, have never crossed the front door. These clothes I put in a suitcase will probably see the light of day for the first time.

Every little action is subject to emotion, "the last time that...", all that I did as a man and that will not happen again.

I did not choose the "classic way" of sex change, if there is one! French law imposes a psychiatric follow-up before starting any treatment whatsoever. The psychiatrist will determine whether or not you suffer from a gender dysphoria, a disorder of identity or any other symptom. The presence of a psychiatrist in the transition process means that gender dysphoria is still considered as a disease. However, in 2013, WHO officially removed it from the list of mental illnesses!

If the psychiatrist gives a favorable opinion, it is possible to consult an endocrinologist who will give access to a hormonal treatment. A two-year psychotherapy is sometimes necessary to obtain the sesame which opens the door of the hormonal treatment. Some more understanding psychiatrists deliver it after one or two sessions ...

Does a homosexual need the advice of a doctor to confirm that he is truly homosexual?

Even though things have moved in recent years, thanks to highly motivated activists and associations, the whole process of sex reassignment requires a unilateral decision by doctors.

In no case would I have accepted a doctor telling me whether or not I could live according to my gender, whether or not I could dispose of my body as I wish. To which other category of people in France does a doctor give permission to live in harmony with oneself? No one!

In other countries, particularly in Asia, anything is possible, especially if you have money... I have been researching for years, studying all aspects of this metamorphosis.
This transition is definitive, the function "cancel" or back does not exist. I know the direction I want to go but the destination is not yet clear. At this point, it is no longer a choice, it is an absolute necessity, the only way out.

My entourage will certainly find it difficult to mourn Christophe, since it is indeed a mourning. Almost a lifetime to be around a man and suddenly hear that this person will become a woman.

When a loved one is sick, we have concerns for them, we worry, we ask ourselves a lot of questions but we will not suffer as much as them.

The family, the friends, the colleagues will undoubtedly have difficulties of acceptance but no one can imagine what represents 48 years of immense sufferings, invisible, hidden, unacknowledged...

How to describe this suffering? A deep pain to not live one's life, to not be understood, to be alone in the world. This pain gnaws even physically, the whole body is affected.

This results in permanent inner anger, deep malaise and self-loathing.

Transgender people are ten times more likely to commit suicide than other populations. Of the transgender youth, 69% thought about suicide, made attempts or did it. It's a real carnage and not much is done to change that.

Why is there no reaction? Why such a reluctance of our politicians to stop this massacre? I hope to be able to do my bit by giving maximum visibility to our cause.

The day will come, I hope, where speaking of transidentity will not be a subject that we will talk about in the media so much it will become "normal" ...When the mind and body do not take the same route, the pain is indescribable.

CHAPTER 1

FOR 53 YEARS, I BELONGED TO HALF OF HUMANITY!

Installed in a sofa, I am here again in this lounge at Hanoi airport. June 1, 2017, well, it's the birthday of my sister Bénédicte.

How many times have I used the chairs in this lounge? Probably more than 50 times since the six years that I live and work in Hanoi. Because of my job, I travel a lot in Japan, China, the USA and Europe. I run a factory producing life jackets, diving suits and this with the help of 420 employees. This job, I love it, running this factory is a pleasure and my team of Vietnamese (in fact, especially Vietnamese women) is very competent. With this level of responsibility, work never stops completely, even during holidays.

Already 12 years of expatriation ... Impossible responsibilities while working in France. Clearly, if you haven't done Harvard or another prestigious school, do not expect to find yourself in a leading team in France. I met many of these people coming in demanding you to explain the right strategy to increase margins. Pretentious just out of school and convinced to belong to an elite, they come with their methods in the American style, the human aspect does not exist, only finance matters. Is this what we learn in these famous schools? No longer considering the value of labor for the benefit of money?

Although having a university degree, I did not go through one of these brilliant schools, for lack of means but especially of will.

On the other hand, I had the chance to enter into Freemasonry at the age of 20, a great school of life, learning to respect others with humanism at the center of all values.

My conception of management puts the worker at the center of the company. Whether it's managers, employees or management, the only goal is to serve production.

My coaching method is based on this principle and it works. Only the worker in front of his machine produces the wealth of the company. Make sure that this worker is fulfilled in his environment, you will get everything you want ... By investing $1 to improve the conditions of the worker, you will get $2 from him. This is certainly not the case in South-East Asia, where the workforce is more likely to be livestock. The worst of it is that it is the local companies, 100% Vietnamese, who treat their workers the worst.

My method works, the results are there, the deliveries are made without delay, of good quality and with good margins.

In an hour, I leave for Bangkok, a trip to the end still uncertain. I'm going to get surgery but I do not know what, nothing is finalized yet. The appointment at Preecha Aesthetic Institute (PAI) is scheduled for 3:30 PM. For months, I compared all the clinics, the different surgeons, collected hundreds of testimonials ... my choice fell on this clinic. The date of return to Hanoi will depend on the appointment of this afternoon, probably in two or three weeks ...

After many e-mails with the clinic, it was agreed to practice hair implants: we take the hairs on the back of the skull and we implant them one by one at the front. A second intervention will consist of the reduction of the Adam's apple, surgery under general anesthesia lasting 20 minutes, nothing really serious even if financially, the cost is not negligible. I want to change this plan, benefit from other surgeries...

A passage to the toilet before boarding. For more than 30 years, I have been watching the entrance next door, the women's washroom. All this time, I thought "One day, I will go through this door! ". It could happen faster than expected, it's my biggest wish.

- *Passengers are called to Gate31!*

A lump forms in my stomach but not because of the anguish of the plane, I'm flying more than four times the earth's circumference per year. Once in the air, it is impossible for me to read or concentrate on anything, I have that in mind, this appointment that will change my life.

CHAPTER 2

IT'S AT THE AGE OF 5-6, for most people who have this disorder, that the first signs appeared. I quickly realized that something was not working properly, I was cataloged in the "man" section while the other one liked me a lot more.

At 6 years, I am convinced, no one else on this planet lives the same thing as me, what I feel is not normal, I have to hide it ... At 5-6 years, I already begin life with unspoken feelings, even lies. Why me?

I will never be a girl, I quickly understood, the magic wand does not exist, what to do? Stop thinking about it! ... It's feasible, no problem ... for a few hours yes, then that need comes back with even more intensity.

We must think about something else but how? Sport, I only see that. First swimming and then running, athletics in summer and finally volleyball. In all these sports, I met successes, departmental champion, regional champion, Alsace team for volleyball, the national championships in running, athletics and volleyball. Good level everywhere but nowhere exceptional.

Added thereafter skiing, tennis and table tennis. Every evening another activity, do not think about it, especially do not think about it ... From primary school to high school, the sport will remain my escape, my buoy.

Every summer, I go to summer camp and this since the age of six, I love going out of the family environment and especially meeting girls. I practice sailing, horse riding, skiing, athletics, tennis, English...

Very early girls interested me, obviously I do not leave them indifferent, the flirts are multiplying ... If I cannot be a girl, what better than to rub shoulders with them?

We live in a tiny village near the German border. This countryside far from everything was chosen to build bars of buildings out of the urban environment. Many migrants settled here, including Portuguese and Moroccans. They arrived with almost nothing, they are completely deprived.

In primary school, clans are formed, not according to the origins but according to the Alsatian dialect spoken or not. Moreover, speaking Alsatian was rigorously forbidden within the school. I do not speak it, my clan is that of francophones, Mum is native from here but Dad comes from Cognac. A compulsory military service in the nearby barracks and here I am with my two youngest sisters.

A large number of foreigners arrived almost overnight in this small village, but I have never witnessed any racism during my childhood.

To overcome their insecurity, my parents collect clothes everywhere, sometimes, the garage is filled with bags ... a real gold mine that I explore during the night. I find dresses and other underwear, I build a reliable secret place in my room. My father is a cabinetmaker, many tools at hand to make a secret hiding place. For short periods, I can feel good, I can be myself, what intensity in those moments. Unfortunately, they are short-lived, I must quickly return to reality.

the fear of being unmasked is terrible, nobody should know or even suspect anything. I need to sacrifice some sleep to get my dose of femininity. It would be so great to just live like that but I know that it strictly impossible.

At 18, I had not spoken to anyone yet and of course, nobody suspects anything. I am tall, muscular, sport has forged a rather great body! How can we imagine for one moment that I want to be a woman?

How to describe this emptiness, this discomfort? The question is always present, throbbing, pernicious: why am I not a girl? This lack is comparable to an addiction such as tobacco, alcohol or drugs. The brain does not claim nicotine but femininity. This translates into wearing women's clothes. Definitely ridiculous to be dressed like that but that's the only way I've found. This weight is heavy to carry, very heavy, it will last until the day of my transition, only temporary fixes possible.

Other questions persist Why me? Why does no one else feel that? I happen to cry, I'm sad but nothing should transpire, no one should know.

At primary school, college and high school, nothing seems really complicated, it bores me more than anything else. I always managed to do the minimum so as not to be bothered and move to the next level without waves. Only sports classes really motivate me, I always had the maximum score, during the exams of the B.A., I was entitled to a 22/20 having exceeded the scales.

Later, I would like to be a sports teacher, anyway, since there is only that which interests me.

My first year in high school, I studied accounting and economy, this section a little catch-all for those who are neither literary nor mathematical. I learn typing, which will be useful all my life. The

Bartholdi school is a wonderful old building named after the famous creator of the Statue of Liberty in New-York, a native of Colmar. building named after the famous creator of the Statue of Liberty in New York, a native of Colmar.

Not really knowing how to orient myself, I'd also learn to work wood like my father. This is an Industrial Technician section in Strasbourg, very little space, I am not accepted. The teachers considered that not being able to work the wood, so why not work the steel, here I am in section T1, the most difficult section in mathematics. I discover milling and filming, it's frankly not my thing, no more than mathematics.

After a most painful year, I come back to my origins with accounting and economy. Why accounting? No idea, a choice like any other.

The following school year, I met Annie. This girl fascinates me, certainly not a supermodel but she has a charm that drives me crazy. At this period, she said libertine ... What does that mean? I have no place in her frivolity at this time.

It does not matter, I have time ... the months pass and little by little, I arrive at my ends, we are together. However, it is not easy to find each other intimately. For our first love meeting, my friend Mathieu welcomes us, a tall fellow who proudly wore a well-stocked beard. It was already a few years since he was with her friend Marianne, it's like they've always been together. Tonight, I'm totally lamentable, such a fear of doing badly cut me all my ways. Obviously, Annie does not look for sex at all costs, I am not disqualified.

At my parents' house, my room is in the basement, Annie comes sometimes to join me through the window, my parents would never accept that she could sleep with me ... but in fact, I never asked them, who know?

Come the period of the exams! As I did not do much during the year, I still open a few books and classes to immerse myself in it but nothing tiresome... Annie is much more serious, prepares sheets, learns by heart ... too hard all that, especially too tiring.

The penalty falls, 13.92 average, at 0,08 points of high honors, I did not hope so much ... I'll console myself with basic honors. Well no, the jury having considered that I had absolutely nothing fucked up the year, they refused me any honor. All this ended with a fantastic arm of honor when leaving high school, the main thing being to have the B.A.

And now what to do? Like any good revolutionary and free thinker, I had to do psychology studies! In fact, I have to do psychology because Annie is doing psychology ... sports teacher, it may well wait a bit.

To gain our independence, we both fill out a form with the rectorate to be supervisors in a middle or high school. Without a boost or labor union, no way to get a job. The director of my former middle school lives in the same street, when I was younger, I sometimes ate at home, their son Vincent having the same age. I explain my case and suddenly, my file is found at the top of the pile at the rectorate and I get a job in my old middle school. On her side, Annie does exactly the same thing with her former middle school and it works. At 18 years, 19 for Annie, we are finally employees, independent and rich ... Between us, we earn more than 11,000 francs which was well above the minimum wage of the time.

To the despair of my parents, we take a studio in Strasbourg 75km away. Long live freedom. Every night we were finally together. It was necessary that I approach the subject, that I explain to her my desires and needs, my pains since childhood. I have never spoken to anyone, I do not know how to do it, what words to use? She does not understand, it's not normal, he may be gay? How to explain to the woman with whom I have just settled down that I need to dress as a woman to feel good? It seems so ridiculous! After much discussion, I can finally wear my first nighty. We discussed it at length with great reluctance on her part but I knew how to convince her. She must see that I remain the same person, I just feel better, myself.

The university, I had to see it 3 or 4 times in the year, working as a supervisor 75km away, but I knew it would not be successful. Moreover, salaried students do not benefit from any development. Happy students who have nothing else to think!

The second year, I get a job in my former high school in Colmar, this time with the help of the union, no choice, no union means no job. At hardly a year after my B.A, I find myself in the same high school ... funny situation.

This is where Freemasonry challenges me, I've read tons of books about it, the more symbolic and abstract to most absurd. It fascinates me and I talk to teachers around me. Until the day, when one of them was put at the disposal to suggest my candidacy in a lodge of the human right. Incredible, having studied all the Freemasonry obedience's, it is the Human Right that I preferred, the only mixed obedience. How to deal without the presence of women?

The procedure starts, three investigators come separately to ask me questions of moral, political, philosophical and symbolic. Three weeks later, I receive a letter of convocation for my Masonic initiation, my candidacy was retained. Each investigator made his report and then the lodge voted by white and black balls, a black ball worth 3 white balls! I do not know how many white balls allowed my admission, but there was enough, that's what matters.

At 20, I am apprentice in the respectable Lodge the Rose and the Square in the East of Colmar (it is the formula consecrated). Only Annie knows, I do not tell anyone else. My parents are believers and Freemasons excommunicated, it is not necessary to refer to it.

As the information of an initiation circulates in the Lodges around all confessions, several people are revealed in my high school which my boss, the headmaster. Overnight, I'm close to the headmaster ... too cool!

Meanwhile, health problems accumulate, knee pain becomes unbearable, too many races, too many marathons, all too young. It is necessary to operate the two ... Evolving at the national level in volleyball, I am entitled to the special treatment of high-level athletes in the orthopedic department of the Colmar hospital. Professor Jaeger is the knee operations guru, all athletes want him. After a quick consultation and an astronomical sum to pay, the date of the intervention is fixed in 3 weeks.

3 weeks later as planned, I go through the admission, fill up tons of documents and move to my room. Marius Tresor and Christian Lopez, who both play in the big soccer team of Les Verts and as well in national team, are on the same floor, this is during the European football cup. I never really liked football but the evenings at 15 in Marius' room, each with its drip and its gallows are downright awesome and allow a little to forget the terrible pain. It is still possible to smoke in the rooms, sometimes the TV seems extinguished so the fog is thick. Some cigarettes have a funny smell, I learn after that it is cannabis. AT 20, I do not even know what it is ... amazing! Difficult end of evenings where each one tries to unravel their IV piping's without tearing them out.

After the knees, pain in the back and sternum become stronger... The pain is such that we must hospitalize me and treat me with morphine. Here I am again in a room of the Pasteur Hospital of Colmar, I will stay a month, it took this time for them to find what disease I suffer. Examinations follow each other, bone scintigraphy of the whole body, very important red areas are visible in the large joints. A karyotype, a chromosome analysis, is performed in order to detect a genetic anomaly. There is a problem on chromosome 6, diagnosed HLA B27, I have ankylosing spondylitis ... thank you doctor, I never heard of this disease. Then the doctor adds:

- *It's funny, you're genetically a woman!*

She finds this funny, in the space of a second, I have the answer to all my questions, those that began at the age of 5, that explains everything. I'm shocked, I'm bowled over, I do not care about spondylitis, I'm a woman!!! Strictly nothing physically shows it but inside, I am a woman, what a comfort. Unfortunately, this will not change anything in everyday life, since I only talked to Annie but it explains so much. I have kept all that to me, since one does not discuss such things.

A small technical explanation from the Internet:

A man is normally built of XY genes and a woman, XX, but there are genetically XX men and women, XY. If it's not a man, then it's a woman. Elementary, my dear Watson ... Hum, not so simple! Nature can also take curious detours and produce in-between. Sometimes the chromosomes say man, but the body says woman ... and vice versa. Although distinct from transsexuality, "sexual reversion" is a purely genetic phenomenon. Man XX is sterile or has an extremely poor production of spermatozoa.

Once the diagnosis of ankylosing spondylitis is confirmed, I can finally leave the hospital accompanied by a treatment with anti-inflammatories and analgesics that I should probably take for life, nothing can cure this disease, just to relieve the effects. This illness is very pernicious, when I wake up in the morning, the pain is so high, I can hardly walk, it takes me 10 minutes to go downstairs. In the evening, I can play a volley-ball match. Nobody can believe that I have so much pain if I can do that in the evening, "he's just putting on a show". It's one more thing that I will hide, I know I'm not credible but the pain is real!

Back in my high school where frankly the job of supervisor does not lead to overwork, the first personal computers are emerging... Beautiful machines, Micral 30, flexible diskettes of 360K and running on MS-DOS and Basic programming language. I am attracted by these screens as by a magnet. I devour all the books that detail operation, after three days I write my first little program.

As soon as I have a free moment, I throw myself on the keyboard, so much so that I am offered to teach computer science. Shop professors are supposed to teach industrial computer courses. Most are close to retirement and have absolutely no desire to approach these devilish machines.

Here I am to give courses in grade 12 and technical college grade, we are the same age but I master the subject, everything is going for the better. I really like that, to teach, I still need to submit a file for my sports teacher project.

Well, imagine that this time is 1984, there are 15 diseases that prohibit you from entering the public service, spondylitis is one of them! Crazy, all my projects fall into the water. I am reorienting towards a diploma in marketing in evening classes, it is even more serious than psychology! The university is in Colmar, no need to make the daily commute. Annie continues the degree in psychology but in correspondence course, too difficult to follow the courses in university, we move to Colmar.

The university courses seem to me of a disconcerting simplicity, I do even less than in high school. The English teacher has a weakness for me, I fly with an average of 15 or 16 on 20. In the absence of a computer teacher, the director of university asks me if I agree to teach it to my class. I am noted on the quality of my courses, I get 19/20. Having not done much, here I am head of my promotion with a university diploma in my pocket.

It's time to think about the serious things, the maximum duration of the supervisor position is reached, a new work is needed, a real one! First interview, first contract, I am a computer trainer for Telmat, a small Alsatian company at the forefront of computer development, perfect! I continue to teach, the national education does not want me, it suits me perfectly.

The height: a few years later, National Education has asked me to kindly teach at the University of Mulhouse and Colmar. I taught at the university for 4 years in large amphitheaters with half of students who had nothing to do with my classes ... until the exams!

Dad, you're so beautiful

CHAPTER 3

1991, ALMOST 10 YEARS OF LIFE TOGETHER WITH ANNIE. Relations are no longer good, yet we decide to do what is necessary to have a child. Stopping the pill, two months later, she's pregnant. With my embarrassment XX, the probability was extremely low, but at that moment I did not know it. Just as I did not know that having no Y factor on chromosome 23, I could only have one girl. A huge joy to learn this pregnancy, at least for me, Annie seems to have difficulties to rejoice ...

The family in which she grew up is not a model of its kind. A former military father, a bullet passed through his skull, alcoholic to the extreme having paid little attention to his four daughters and son. Incredible but true, his name is Julius Caesar.

Her mother never leaves her apron, constantly looking for something to polish. insults constantly fly between dear spouses, he does not leave his TV and his bottle, she does not leave her kitchen... What a life, what a waste.

At 6 months of pregnancy, doctors realize that the baby is no longer growing, stress, anxiety. An amniocentesis is performed to detect a possible trisomy. Nothing, there is nothing, no plausible reason. To increase the anxiety, the first contractions appear.

At 26 weeks, hospitalization with complete immobilization is required. The contractions are under control but the baby is still not growing. At seven and a half months, the medical team suggests a caesarean, there is no evolution for days.

The baby is low birth weight and has stopped growing without our understanding the reasons. Immobilization allows the fetus to continue developing vital organs, especially the lungs.

The day before the intervention, the neonatology staff made me discover the service and the room of resuscitation where will be welcomed our child.

It is a girl, I am 100% convinced, I impose more or less the first name Anaïs. A beautiful name filled with sweetness. No male first name is chosen.

The obstetrician was very clear, it's 50/50, the baby's survival is really not certain, to my surprise I am offered to attend the cesarean section. The only condition is:

- *If you fall, we will not pick you up!*

Of course! I will participate but I do not sleep at night, however, I cannot imagine for a moment that it can go wrong.

26 March 1991 at 9:30 AM, Annie is installed on the operating table, I hold her hand ... She is completely in a daze and does not really realize what is happening. The medical team seems relaxed, Enya's soft voice resonating in the room is certainly contributing.

I look at the beginning of the procedure, incision, intestines placed next to the belly, it is time to look away. A few minutes later, Anaïs makes her appearance and makes us enjoy her voice. It seems that everything is going well, Annie is not aware of anything, we have a daughter.

I find myself with the surgeon in the locker room to remove the sterile clothes, another doctor arrives:

- *What did you get? A taco or a sausage?*
- *A taco, I present you the father*

A way to decompress but that made me laugh, I needed it. The presence of fathers in the block is not very common.

Two hours later, I return to the sterile resuscitation room where Anaïs is, 1,080 kg, barely more than a packet of sugar, she holds in one hand. The machines do not frighten me, any more than all the connections on this small body, she has my full attention, I look at her again and again, I speak to her, I touch her. I stay more than an hour when suddenly the machines emit terrible beeps, as in the movies, a line replaces the heartbeat. I take her in my right hand, shake her and talk to her. It goes away, the heart is gone ... The nurses come running, it was a close call.

The next day, I learn that I served as a test subject. During the visit of the service the day before the birth, I was filmed. When I arrived to see my daughter, they did the same. Being familiar with all the machinery, I focused only on my daughter, nothing else and that saved her. From then on, the service visit was systematic for all parents.

Annie is very bad, she feels guilty, see our daughter makes her suffer. After a few days, Annie leaves the hospital but Anaïs stays there. The weight goes under the kilo, we cheat at the weighing so that she is not transferred to Strasbourg.

Every day we come to see her, bathe her, feed her. Holding this baby in the palm of the hand, following the evolution of her weight with anguish, some moments are difficult to manage.

My parents can only see her through a window, neonatology is only available to parents to limit the risk of viral transmission to these tiny creatures. It will take weeks for her to reach 2.5kg and she can leave this establishment that has taken care of her so well.

Here she is finally at home, we are parents, a family.

Soon we realize that Anaïs has developmental delays. A lot of exams are performed, several doctors examine her but we find nothing, no explanation.

She evolves at her own pace, she smiles and laughs constantly, what more?

Anaïs will not see me dressed as a woman, it seems obvious. My moments of well-being are becoming rarer, this lack weighs more and more in my relationship with Annie who does not accept me in the same way, it becomes a simple tolerance then a rejection. Comes the day of the ultimatum:

- *You heal yourself or we separate. You have to go see a shrink, I do not give you the choice!*

Against my will, I make an appointment at the psychiatric center of Rouffach. A young psychologist, probably in her thirties, oversees assessing the extent of the damage. For the first time I talk about my "problem", I explain how much it weighs on me and makes me suffer. I do not choose anything, I suffer, the more I resist, the more the pain increases.

At my surprise, I am diagnosed sexual deviant, my attitude is not socially acceptable. She demolished me, destroys me, I never imagined falling so low. I am proposed to follow an experimental drug protocol. At the risk of affecting my relationship with Annie, I refuse. I am a woman genetically, how could drug change that?

For the first time, the idea of suicide is present and more and more persistent. Never again will I see a shrink, these pseudo experts who decide, with a bewildering aplomb, to diagnose me as sexual deviant. The purpose of the speech is to convince you of the sexual disease to better treat it ... In addition, it is a psychologist, she is not even a doctor! Rouffach Psychiatric Hospital ... never again!

The crucial choice is necessary, after 12 years of living together, we separate.

CHAPTER 4

1ST OF JUNE 2017, this one-and-a-half-hour flight lasted an eternity. The airport of Bangkok has no secret, I soon reach the meeting point. I see a poster with my name held by the one who will be my driver.

45 minutes' drive to Thonglor, the Japanese quarter of the Thai capital. The clinic is very small, a building of 3 floors, I was expecting something more imposing. Once inside, it's a mix of zany and coarse. Did I do well to choose this clinic?

Boys at the front desk are busy in all directions with exaggerated manners, they call everyone darling and make ridiculous kisses with every turn.

A Thai woman, probably an advanced age, wait for her turn? Her face of wax completely frozen still shows the same grin. How can we get here? Is this eternal youth? How awful.

I see a Westerner, probably an American given of his rather imposing corpulence. What kind of surgery can he need? At the call of his name, I understand that the surgery is already done. He gets up and retrieves his red buoy. He / she just had surgery, I do not perceive the slightest feminine trait, neither in clothes nor in attitude. Plus, he does not look happy at all.

At next to him sits another trans, quite the opposite, breasts disproportionate visible, an ultra-short skirt, heels of a vertiginous height, a parody of the woman, vulgarity in its pure state. I'm suddenly scared, could I become one of those two creatures?

I just want to be invisible, that nobody pays attention to me, that I can live according to my gender, nothing more.

I fill in the usual forms, I wait about fifteen minutes then comes my turn to meet Dr. Sutin. He is probably in his fifties, much taller than the Thai average, a good appearance, probably a handsome man:

- *Well, you come today for hair implants and for the Adam's apple reduction. Obviously, your hair is poor, even in the back, not sure that the results are very conclusive. I would advise you at first to realize the face feminization in order to lower the line of hair by 2 cm and then the hair implants.*

That's exactly what I wanted, moving the planned operations in September to do them now.

- *No problem but if my face changes, it is necessary that my sex changes at the same time!*

I could not imagine appearing as a "woman" in everyday life and keeping my male sex. Some transgender people are quite capable of assuming their femininity by keeping their male sex, I fully respect it but personally, I am unable. French and Thai law requires living in his new gender at least a year before proceeding to the sexual reassignment. This is not my case and I categorically refuse to impose this kind of thing, too bad, I will lie.

Dad, you're so beautiful

- *I will see if Dr. Burin would be available for this operation!*

Dr. Sutin leaves his office, my heart must beat at 150bpm, I'm hot, very hot. The wait is endless, it must work ... It gets hotter, it lasts, it lasts ... He comes back, the heart goes to 200bpm ...

- *That's fine, Dr. Burin will do the sexual reassignment while I make your face. We will operate the day after tomorrow morning.*

YES ... Two days to D-day!!! That's it, the dice are thrown, the tears are rising, tears of joy.
Dr. Sutin explains the details are FFS procedure (face feminization surgery) accompanied by very explicit drawings he makes by skilled free hand.

We make an incision starting from one ear, we follow the line of hair to the other ear, the skin will be folded down on the lower face in order to plane the orbital bone just under the eyebrows. The hairline will drop 2 cm by pulling very hard on the whole skin of the skull, the eyebrows will be raised one centimeter and a complete facelift will be done. I should look 10 years younger ...

10 years younger, this is not the goal, I just want to look feminine, regardless of my age. I will never be a supermodel, I just want to become a woman like any other, nothing more.

Dr. Burin is much more taciturn, he seems almost shy. I undress, the size of the penis will define the depth of the vagina, no worries.

- *Your vagina will be about 15cm deep*

Ok, I had never looked at this question, for the moment, it's really the last of my worries.

If the penis is too small, which happens frequently with Asians, it is necessary to take a piece of intestine which will serve as a vagina, a much heavier surgery and of course more expensive. There are many trans in Thailand, the famous ladyboys ... which will have enough money to pay for such a surgery?

He then shows me pictures explaining the different stages of the surgery. You need to be strong to see these images, I have seen and reviewed dozens of times, I know by heart the different stages of the construction of the vagina, clitoris and vulva ... As long as the result is at the rendezvous ...

This rendezvous, it is scheduled for Saturday, June 3, I have the end of the afternoon and all day tomorrow to complete all necessary exams.

The clinic is not equipped for this kind of surgery, which reassures me, I did not see anything that looked like an operating room, a recovery room or even rooms.

Surgeries are practiced at the hospital Piyavate ... The establishment is huge, probably more than twenty floors on a very large floor space. Impressive modernity, organization, cleanliness and quality of service, that I have never seen in France. Blood tests, chest x-ray, electrocardiogram, endocrinologist, anesthesiologist ... I go from one wicket to another, from one examination room to another, a nurse guides me into this anthill.

I am exhausted, happy but also worried that I can find my hotel in the evening. Tomorrow, the cardiologist will decide whether or not I can be operated on. In the afternoon, I will see two psychiatrists who, I hope, will give me the precious pass for the life I am waiting for.

I go to the bar and enjoy a cocktail, I who have not drunk alcohol for two years, my god it's good. However, the buffet is more than average, but today it really doesn't matter ...

The procedures that can take years in France are settled in 2 days in Thailand. Clearly, the clinic has every interest in the surgeries being done, since $ 24,000 is at stake.

Dad, you're so beautiful

CHAPTER 5

IN BANGKOK, IN MY ROOM, thousands of questions cross my mind, feelings of immense joy and anguish mingle ... In two days, I will finally be a woman. I am alone, so alone, yet I am married to Jeannette.

My dear wife left me a few weeks ago when I informed her of this appointment in Bangkok.

We were going to celebrate our 20th wedding anniversary, 20 years together with highs and lows, I was happy, now, I'm not sure she was.

In 1996, during our first meeting, she worked as a waitress in a restaurant where we go after volleyball training. She has class, very elegant and an incredible presence !!! the age difference is 14 years, I'm 32, she's 46, I do not care, anyway I've always preferred mature women! We go out in the mountains and share our first kiss. The second appointment is only for hugs, we will not go further. It was at the third appointment, including the attraction I felt for this woman that I tell her about my situation and my irrepressible need to feel like a woman. I cannot imagine starting a relationship and hiding permanently the woman who lives deep within me.

She understands and says she accepts the situation. Really? unbelievable!!! And it's true, I introduce myself to her wearing skirt and blouse and everything is going well... Never had I hoped so much. Very quickly, I settle in her apartment, everything works perfectly. Jeannette is divorced and lives alone with her 17-year-old daughter. Cohabitation is going pretty well, especially since she goes to see her father every other weekend, which gives us moments just for us.

Very quickly, we undertake to restore her birthplace, an old house on the mountainside just at the foot of the Vosges. Absolutely everything has to be redone, all the walls, all the floors, all the ceilings, the electricity, the heating, everything, everything ... It's my dream, like in sport, I'm not a master of any skill but I can do a little of all trades. I have the advantage of seeing things finished before starting them. I know exactly each process that will achieve the goal.

We work almost day and night, after a few months, we settle in the house in a precarious way to no longer waste time on the move.

A year has passed, we can finally enjoy our new home. Our financial means are really limited, it is certain that by appealing to professionals, the result would have been more pleasant but it came from us, from our hands, we would not have wanted someone else to do it.

Jeannette was born and raised in this house, an old farm with cows and pigs. A tough education punctuated by the seasons and their respective tasks. It is not necessary to beg her to get to work, she is extremely valiant, it is sometimes difficult to stop her.

When the marriage arrived, it seemed obvious to me to make my life with this woman. For my birthday, she offers me a beautiful white satin nightgown with her bathrobe. Beyond the beauty of the product, it is the beauty of the gesture that matters to me, I am really in heaven, being able to dress at will in our intimacy.

The party is a real success, all the family and friends are there. Jeannette is hypersensitive, even more than me, tears do not cease to flow throughout the day. She did not think to remarry one day.

She is now a saleswoman in a bakery, I still work in the same computer company by varying the responsibilities. Training, I became after-sales service manager and then software project manager, I get my status as an engineer.

Comes the beginning of the internet, Telmat is at the forefront in this field, we were the first to send a message to Poland via an X25 line and we received an answer the next day! We were the pioneers of the internet in France. You realize the speed, in 24 hours, we had feedback. Today, it looks like prehistory.

The internet is becoming more and more important; the information highways are on the front pages of all newspapers. Website programming is becoming my main area of activity. It mixes creativity for the look of the site and programming, great, I love it.

I create my first personal site on Geocities where I speak of Celine, my double, the one who lives in the anonymity of our household. This name, I had chosen when I was 12 years old, I dreamed that one could call me like that one day, a beautiful name. It's probably a famous French song that made me love this name. It's through the internet that I finally understood that I was not the only one to live this, thousands of men were in the same situation all over the world ... Overnight, we could communicate, just incredible!

Quickly, I decided to go on an adventure and I created my website development company, Archinet, "the architects of the internet". A little reminder to my Masonic membership!

I work day and night, I do small websites, demand is important and my creativity is appreciated. The Markstein ski resort is only 10 minutes from my home, I often go skiing on weekends or at night. However, at 1200 meters altitude, the amount of snow is rather capricious. If only it was possible to see the snow on the slopes before climbing

While searching, I find manufacturers of cameras in the USA, they can be connected directly to a modem, that's exactly what I need. Over time, the owners of the resort have become my friends. I installed two cameras that take one image per hour, sent to a server by a communication between two 56K modems, incredible, it works ... As a pioneer in France in this area, the local newspaper Alsace published an article with photos, then Europe 1 (main French radio) contact me for an interview, then comes the turn of radios RTL and NRJ, then TV with France 3 and TF1.

Within days, everyone in the region knows me, opening my doors for more important projects such as Clairefontaine notebooks, Jacob Holm, Villiger, Schlumberger ...I'm overloaded, even working 20 hours a day, I cannot. I need to find help for the sales side in order to be able to devote myself to programming. This is the beginning of the end, I hired the wrong people, the controls do not fit anymore. I have reacted too late, my mistake, and bankruptcy.

Jeannette lives it very badly, it's the end of the world, especially since you have to make a loan to pay off debts.

The fall is difficult, she no longer looks at me the same way, something broke. Quite quickly, I find work in a computer company, I am responsible for a PC assembly unit.

At second floor is the company Sevylor: all my youth. Inflatable pools, air mattresses, inflatable kayaks that I hung on the back of the bike ... A dream, if only I could work on it.

By successive approaches, I meet Robert, the General Manager. Older than me, always smiling and cordial, the current goes well. I tell him about my experience and my passion for this company.

At the same time, I do a lot of paintings and pastels, I love that. I participated to small exhibitions in all regional parties, I sell some canvases time to time which making nice pleasure.

It was Angèle and François, a sister and a brother of my lodge, who launched me. We meet every Sunday, François teaches us to draw, Angèle prepares sumptuous meal. Soon, painting becomes a passion, I install a workshop at home that allows me to not have to tidy up every time I leave my canvas. Later, I discover the pastel, the works of Degas, I make copies then my own paintings. The realization is much faster, no drying time and work on the sheet is done with the fingers. The magic of colors at the end of his fingers, much better than brushes. At an exhibition where we were asked to be in action in front of the visitors, everyone has the same thought:

- *Haaa, you do that with your fingers.*

My exasperated neighbor after a whole day of hearing the same thing suddenly bursts:

Dad, you're so beautiful

- *You can see that he's using fingers, he does not do that with his dick ...*

We are obviously bent of laughing. My painting is rather surrealistic, Dali style. During these shows, I hear so many silly comments that I stop participating

- *You see, on this canvas, the artist wanted to say that ...*

I do not want to say anything at all and how can you know better than me?

Sevylor is part of the Zodiac group. The image of leisure conveyed by Sevylor is no longer compatible with the seriousness that Zodiac wants to show its shareholders. They decide to sell Sevylor to his main Chinese supplier: Michael Lee ... The company will become Chinese, incredible. A so prosperous company just after the war, a pioneer in its field, it is in the hands of the Chinese.

I should not complain, I got this job through this sale to set up a new ERP, the complete IT management system with branches in Germany, Belgium and Italy.

At my hiring, Robert was clear:

- *You will be responsible to install this system, to operate it in all units. Once everything works, I would like you to take care of all the research and development for Sevylor, I saw your paintings and I think that you will be able to be the person we need. You leave in 15 days for China, you must understand the manufacturing process!*

How to refuse such an offer, nothing like this kind of challenge to motivate me ... I took dozens of domestic flights when I worked for Telmat. For the first time, I will take an international flight to Hong Kong, I do not even know where it is!

Stress, before departure, how will I be able to stay more than 12 hours on a plane without smoking?

I am accompanied by Gérard, a retired engineer who worked for Zodiac several decades. A kind of genius with several patents to his credit, a vast culture. He set up all the production processes in the Chinese factory. He has only one big defect: he is void in language, he needs a translator permanently.

Gerard will be my mentor for several years, it is him who will teach me all the technical parts necessary to make sure the products that I create hold the road.

The time of departure has come, we are three: Robert the boss, Gerard the pensioner and me. We arrive at Paris CDG by taking a flight Mulhouse-Paris, barely 50 minutes.

In Terminal E, I discover for the first time the lounge reserved for gold members or business class travelers. We travel in economics but I am invited in the lounge by Robert who has the Gold status. When the moment of boarding arrives, Robert negotiates at the entrance of the lounge for a possible upgrade, Gerard is Platinum ... I am nothing. Here we are all three upgraded to Business Class, incredible, I will make my first long distance flight in very good conditions. This was the time when individuals could still decide on an upgrade and not the machines like now.

We land at the new airport in Hong Kong, it seems that the old was terrible, it needed a special license to pilots to land, one of the most complicated and dangerous landings, the buildings are only a few meters of the wings. Videos are still available on the internet, I'm happy to avoid that.

The trip goes without any problem, I am comfortable and sleep for several hours. As soon as the doors open, the smell so characteristic of Asia fills the cabin. Hong Kong is still under British tutelage, we must take the ferry to China mainland. Immigration and luggage, we head for the ferry that will take us to Shenzhen, there is no direct flight between Paris and Canton. At the Chinese border, I'm not reassured, it takes almost an hour to finally get out of this sordid building. My visa is in order, here I am for the first time in China. A driver is waiting for us outside the building, he knows Robert and Gerard well.

I discover the first landscapes of China, factories, dormitories, as far as the eye can see. The landscape remains the same over tens of kilometers. In places, there are electric poles planted at 40 meters height. The hill has been completely devoured all around to make it a flat building soil. Obviously, nothing stops them.

The factory is in Guangdong Province, in the south of China, one hour thirty drive form the border. The highway is quite uncrowded but it runs anyway. The "village" where is implanted the factory still has a million inhabitants: a village on the scale of China.

The foreigners are few, only the two hotels 5 stars (Chinese) allow you to see some of them. Our hotel is the Sun City, a very thick red carpet that smells like mold, a huge reception, the same music that runs in a loop, almost nobody speaks English. We are a curiosity for these Chinese who look at us as extraterrestrials and laugh a lot in our back ... Not so easy to get used to!

We finally arrive at the factory, a shabby place behind a large green metal gate, several dilapidated buildings rub shoulders. I meet Michael Lee, the owner of the factory and the new owner of Sevylor, a native Chinese whose parents fled to Taiwan at the time of Chang kai Chek. He must be in his sixties, thin and long, he seems puny and very fragile. We discuss ... finally Robert discusses again and again, I would so much like to visit this factory and finally understand. I have always been fascinated by the manufacturing process, I prefer to visit a factory than a museum ...

Gerard finally takes me to discover the different floors, workers look at us from head to toe, it's curious to feel this weight on my shoulders. All products are made of PVC, I visit the workshop cutting, screen printing, welding, sewing ... The welds are made by huge high frequency machines, I do not understand everything but it is the main workshop that counts dozens of these machines of all sizes...

Everything looks dirty, old, and yet I learn that the factory is only 5 years old. The materials must be of very poor quality, incredible, these buildings seem to be over 30 years old, I do not even dare to imagine the state of the canteen. I take my first Chinese meal in a separate room, I fight with my chopsticks. The chopsticks are like skiing, you must never cross! The flavors are new, it's not my cup of tea, I hope it will not eat every day this way! We stay the whole week at the factory, Gerard takes all his time to explain to me, to teach me. I absorb all this with a lot of greed, I ask for more.

Back in France, I have tons of things to tell, it is not commonplace to talk about China when you live in a tiny village of 400 people.

Robert understood my interest and especially saw how fast I learn; the trips will be repeated. The third trip is directly to

Canton (Guangzhou), Air France has finally opened a direct flight. The procedures are much simpler and especially faster.

On this trip, Michael Lee informs us that he has decided to move the factory to Shanghai ... That seems much more interesting.

A year has passed with several other trips to southern China. Finally, the first trip to Shanghai, we were looking forward to it. Shanghai is not China, far from it, it is a megalopolis of 25 million inhabitants that is more modern, nothing like the Guangdong countryside. Shanghai is beautiful, the city is dressed in light as soon as night falls, banal buildings during the day become magnificent bright pyramids at night. There is so much to discover, to visit, to taste and to learn. In Shanghai, no one pays attention to the alien circulating.

The factory is brand new, Michael Lee is very proud to introduce us to it. Gerard looks at all the machines, the different workshops, he has probably already seen a hundred things to correct.

What a contrast to the previous factory ... In Guangdong, the rats circulated everywhere, they were an integral part of the factory, nobody paid attention, even Gerard no longer looked at them. In Shanghai, everything is clean, orderly, floors washed, all machines have a protective cover, what a contrast!

Future trips between France-China are scheduled one after the other, I spend more and more time in the factory, Gérard is no longer on all trips, I acquired a certain technical independence but still very far from knowing enough of it, I am convinced that Gerard still has many things to teach me.

Besides, he does not hide his pleasure to share his know-how. I work mainly with the research and development team for the creation of new products and for the improvement of others, our main client is Decathlon. More and more often, Michael asks me to look at manufacturing processes more closely and improve them. I do not have an industrial background but I realize that the simple logic is often sufficient. It always amazed me in China: if at a toll booth you have a line of two trucks and another line of ten cars, they will always go to the shortest, the line with ten cars, they will wait five times longer!

At every trip, we spend a few days in the south to visit our other suppliers. At the end of each day, we are invited for dinner in a very chic restaurant, we always have a room just for us with the traditional round table featuring a lazy-Susan. These meals are accompanied with cognac or whiskey, we must show that we know how to receive and that we do not look at the expense. The gānbēi (one go toasts) follow one another, the Chinese are completely drunk, we are not far from joining them.

The evening continues at Karaoke. The Mama San, the hostess, installs us in a room with huge benches, small tables, several microphones and a large TV. Come in twenty girls, each of us must choose the one that suits him. What a horror, how to point a finger and say: "I want this one", it's like being in a market. They wear evening dresses, they are beautiful. They take care of filling the glasses, they play dice, sing ... until all disappear when the evening comes to an end. Ten minutes later, they come back in street clothes, jeans, sport shoes ... what a contrast, it is the moment to negotiate the continuation, that means going in the room.

Gerard had warned me, they are insistent but he used to dodge their charms, we return to our rooms, alone. These are kids and more, the amount of alcohol ingested would not do much!

Michael has more and more problems with Conny, the president of Sevylor in the United States as well as with Robert ... He realizes that he does not control them, everyone wants to do his own way. Tired of constant disputes, misplaced egos, he decided to sell all the activity to a big American group: K2.

The plant is now under the responsibility of Stearns, the US leader in lifejackets and inflatable kayaks. The CEO, Paul, and Chief Financial Officer Mike, come twice to evaluate the plant and audit as part of a group integration.

During their second visit, Paul asks me the question:

- *We have observed you, we have appreciated your abilities and your financial knowledge, you are best placed to run this factory, what do you think?*

The shock, I am asked to become General Manager of a factory that has 650 workers and realizes $ 15 million in turnover ... After all, there are not so many people who have the skills and who are ready to come live in China.

Gerard had told me on the fourth trip:

- *One day, you will be in charge of this factory, that's for sure!*

For his part, my boss Robert had told me:

- *Do not make any illusion, you will never run this factory!*

Well, it's Gerard who won. I had hoped, I had expected and now I'm thrilled. I phone Jeannette to tell her the news ... Even if we had not spoken openly, we knew that the request could occur. To make 12 to 13 trips a year became absolutely exhausting and the absences unbearable.

On the phone, without any hesitation, Jeanette accepts immediately. An expatriation only succeeds if the spouse agrees. The package was really interesting: a salary multiplied by three, two return tickets each year, accommodation, a personal driver and a cleaning lady ... Hard to refuse such an offer.

The same day, I confirm to Paul, the CEO of Stearns, that I accept their proposal. The dice are thrown, we are in 2006 and are going to leave for an expatriation of undefined duration, and this on the other side of the planet.

The next day, I start visiting apartments and houses in a very particular area of Shanghai. It is inconceivable that we live in a tower, we have always lived in a house. The choices were therefore oriented towards the villas. I knew there was a golf club in downtown Hong Qiao and I always had the dream of practicing this sport, so I looked around ...

It does not take long to find a beautiful villa in Hong Mei Lu street. 3 floors, 4 bedrooms and 4 bathrooms ... just across from the golf course, I will just have to cross the road, hard to beat. At 1 km away is the largest Carrefour store in China, there is really everything.

We will move and Jeannette will discover what will be her future home. I go back to France to help her pack and close the house ... Going on vacation is one thing, leaving for expatriation is a different one ...

The day before we leave, I go to my doctor to fill up on drugs for my Ankylosing Spondylitis ... I need at least for 6 months medication. She takes me the blood pressure as usual, the figures explode, 180/110 of tension when I never exceeded the 120/80. She listens to me, she quickly realizes a problem by palpating my neck. She discovers a significant outgrowth. I had felt a discomfort swallowing but I had not seen this bump in my neck.

The same day, ultrasound is irrevocable: important thyroid nodules on both sides. Additional examinations will be necessary especially to check if there is cancer ...

The eve of departure ... Damn, it's not possible, again something wrong!

There is no question of changing the plans, we go to Shanghai as planned and we will see later for the thyroid.

Jeannette discovers this new megalopolis as well as her new home. Leaving a village of 400 inhabitants to end up in a city of 25 million people, we can call it a change of scenery. The city is sumptuous, so much to discover, to visit. You must relearn everything: how to move, how to communicate, discover the price of things, find something to eat ... Other French live in the same residential area, they are a great help to exchange addresses and give advice.

Driving at night in Shanghai is a spectacle all by itself, all these illuminated towers, with architecture so different and bold. The main point of view of Shanghai is the Bund, located in the chic and trendy district, it gives an unobstructed view of Pudong and its towers. The television tower in the form of balls connected to each other lights up at nightfall, it's so kitsch but impressive anyway. Next door are the two largest towers in China. The highest is called the bottle opener because of its opening in a rectangle at the top.

Life is beautiful and easy, housekeeper, private driver, increased financial means, what more can you ask for. We are in the ecstasy experienced by all expats during the first six months.

Jeannette quickly finds girlfriends, she has this ability to attract sympathy, we start to go out, meet people. We are invited to the left and right then we invite ... We discover this famous expat community, all these women who complain about their cleaning lady or their driver, these women who had none of these in France. These French high school teachers who know better than anyone how to run a factory. All those people who complain about the Chinese:

But go back to France, of course we do not have the same culture but we are guests in this country, you're free to leave if you are not satisfied.

Fortunately, there are some interesting people, we are a small group of five couples with the same affinities. It's still incredible that big business leaders are the simplest and the most interesting people. They do not have swollen egos, they know how to work with the Chinese ... We quickly become accomplices and go out every weekend, finally good times far from all this French community!

Dad, you're so beautiful

CHAPTER 6

BANGKOK JUNE 2, 2017, D-DAY -1 BEFORE THE SURGERIES, this day will be decisive, it is the cardiologist and the two psychiatrists who will decide my future. The sun seems never to rise. By consulting my emails, I discover that Jeannette contacts all my relatives by trying to convert them to her cause. She who for twenty years lived next to a woman in intimacy does not support that I can live it finally in broad daylight. How far will she go to stop me from living my life, she who said: "whatever you do, I will follow you". Naively I believed it. My parents, my sister support me ... fortunately.

In the morning, I will return to Piyavate Hospital to meet the cardiologist and a nephrologist. The cardiologist will decide whether or not the surgery can be performed, this visit is mandatory for people over 45 years old.

Once finished, it will be necessary to change hospital to meet the two psychiatrists.

Boun, the customer manager of the clinic advises me to make up and look as feminine as possible.

- *Psychiatrists take more account of appearance than anything else.*

In the space of half an hour, the doctor will get an idea about the person and will sign the famous "open sesame" giving access to the surgeries, what an insult to their art!!!

I wear makeup as best as I can, this is the first time I will appear in public ... A very low-neck T-shirt, a white satin cropped pants and small sandals recently bought ...

I go down to the lobby of the hotel, no driver at the moment. Nobody pays attention to me, I move, I cross, I sit, I feel good ... so good! My God, am I really going to be able to live this happiness every day?

Arrived at the hospital, a nurse takes me to the cardiologist's office who I met the day before. He talks in Thai with this nurse, obviously there is something that does not please him in the electrocardiogram done the day before ... Oh no, not yet a new problem!

To dispel this doubt, he wants me to do an ECG monitoring under effort. Another review, will it never end? On the other hand, it shows the seriousness with which they treat patients, it is not the commercial aspect that takes over.

Before this exam, I meet the nephrologist. The blood test showed a too high potassium levels, the cause is the anti-androgen drug that blocks the production of male hormones. I should have stopped my hormonal treatment two weeks before the surgery but then, I was leaving for hair implants, not for a vaginoplasty!

His English is pitiful, I try to explain to him my heavy medical baggage, my ankylosing spondylitis, anti-inflammatories, analgesics and hormonal treatment that I swallow daily. He does not understand anything, what an idiot he can only say to me:

- *You know, you should not take these drugs, it's not good!*

He's clueless, as if I took these drugs by pure pleasure for more than 30 years. I give up, I abound in its direction hoping to complete this ordeal as soon as possible.

Fourth blood test then I return to cardiology. In a locker room, I'm equipped with a tracksuit, socks and sneakers towards the treadmill. I'm plugged on all sides, the chest, arms and then the treadmill starts... slowly, then faster and faster: my breasts are walking in all directions, what a strange and very pleasant feeling. Knees start to burn, the rhythm is really strong, I see that the needles of the printer panic ... stoooooop ... The machine stops, I cannot take it anymore, I'm sweating so much.

I go back to get dressed, my makeup is now fucked, I hope to have a moment to rewrap my nose before seeing the psychiatrists.

Before that, I see the cardiologist for the results of the last exam, if he puts his veto, no need to continue. How would I react if that was the case? He reviews the different pages of the ECG, we see clearly the pulsations tighten as he turns them. His conclusion is without appeal.

- *Miss, you have a teenage heart!*

A huge sigh of relief, what better wish? By appreciating in passing the use of the feminine. A huge weight dissipates instantly ... I passed all medical examinations, it remains to meet the psychiatrists ...

After a quickly swallowed sandwich and an express facelift, we head to another hospital to consult the two psychiatrists.

I'm sitting in the waiting room, I'm waiting an hour and a half for the first appointment. Other girls come before me, all Thai. They also want to look feminine, they look more like prostitutes. I am hard with these girls because very few women would dress that way in town, let alone to consult a psychiatrist. What kind of woman they want to look like? A very sad image, to wonder if I'm in a brothel or a hospital? It is not surprising that the image of transgender people is so bad.

I enter the tiny office of the first psychiatrist. She is Thai, in her thirties, she seems to be bored, not the slightest expression on her face. My hairs are relaxed on the side and go over my shoulder, the neckline clearly visible, I adopt a feminine position without exaggeration.

Since when do you feel that you are a woman? Since when do you live permanently as a woman?

The Thai law imposes a minimum of one year of public life in the new gender. I must improvise, lie. I tell her that my impulses started from an early age, this need to dress and feel woman whenever I could. I say I have lived this way for 15 months and everyone is aware of my future transition. The shrink is fixed on my breasts, a good C cup, she does not take their eyes off them.

- *When did you start the hormones and do the breast implants?*
- *I started to take hormones 2 years ago, on the other hand my breast is completely natural.*

She does not return, fixes them even more. The interview lasted twenty minutes to maximum after which I get a certificate stating that I suffer from gender dysphoria and that nothing prevents proceeding with sex reassignment surgery.

Same thing for the second shrink, in 15 min the interview ends ... Boun had told me so: the external aspect counts more than the lived experience of each person.

Transitioning to 53 years of age means thinking for decades. At 20, the risks of being wrong, of not making the right choice, are much higher. These Thais have beautiful bodies but what opportunities they have besides prostitution, massage parlors or cabaret? I do not hold it against them. I suppose that for psychiatrists, to allow such a request to a person of 53 years represents a low risk, moreover, I am a foreigner and I will not stay in the country. I could of course have done this step earlier but I do not regret having waited all this time. This is the right moment, I'm ready.

The consultations are over, I'm on my way back to the hotel, this day has been particularly long and fraught with anguish and emotion. It is done, I have the green light of all the doctors ... No more obstacles in my way. Tomorrow I will be a woman!!! Just to think about it, tears of happiness flood my face ...

Dad, you're so beautiful

CHAPTER 7

2008 IN SHANGHAI, for two years we settled in the Chinese economic capital, an easy expatriate life, very pleasant with the opportunity to discover a new culture. My job suits me perfectly, I control the factory well and the financial results prove it. This level of income changes lives, not worrying about month end is one of the largest luxuries.

I practice golf almost daily, practicing sessions every night and courses on weekends, sometimes on weekdays very early. In summer, the heat quickly becomes overwhelming, I play at 5 in the morning, nobody on the course, just my caddy and me.

Yet one morning very early, I see police cars and buses parked at the departure of the golf course, it is 5 am, what happens? An old man starts playing right in front of me, his game is mediocre, he is accompanied by a court that applauds the slightest of his gestures ... so ridiculous. He has big square glasses and a fixed smile; his police escort is consistent. I just started my Chinese lessons, my caddy tries to explain to me:

- *Zhōngguó dì yı ge! Chinese number one ... I do not understand anything.*

After a few holes, we play together, I am also entitled to shy applause. His English is as mediocre as his game, I make him understand that I am French and live here, nothing more. We finish our 9 holes by shaking hands.

It's only a few months later, watching the Chinese Communist Party's 60th anniversary ceremonies, that I discover my fellow sitting next to the current president. I played with Jiang Zemin, former Chinese president. For the employees of the factory, I became the one who played with the President! The cult of the person is part of Chinese propaganda.

About health, my goiter becomes extremely visible, it spreads on the whole right side of the neck, going towards the nape of the neck. The surgery cannot be postponed anymore, this thyroid causes collateral effects such as hypertension, sleep disorder, aggressiveness, excitement and weight loss.

It took two years and the insistence of the embassy doctor that I decided to seek treatment. During a previous trip to France, I underwent a series of exams at the hospital, including the injection of a radioactive product to perform a scintigraphy.

Terrifying to see this logo representing the radioactivity and the precautions that the nurses take to inject me! The examination confirms a hot nodule, which frankly leaves me perplexed. It seems that a cold nodule is more often subject to cancer, a hot nodule must be less bad.

November 12, 2008, Pasteur Hospital of Colmar, surgery department, I am admitted for a planned surgery during my previous trip. My thyroid gland has grown quite improbable, almost preventing me from eating so much pressure on the esophagus is important.

I left Shanghai two days ago, a surgery of this type is unthinkable in China. Jeannette stayed in our villa in Shanghai, this small surgery does not justify paying a plane ticket.

Dr. Charles Meyer is the specialist in the thyroid gland. Great practice is required to perform this sensitive surgery. The doctor explains in detail the process of intervention, he is confident and reassuring while informing me of the potential risks such as internal hemorrhage, but only in one case out of 200,000.

The day before the surgery, the anesthesiologist assesses my medical history, allergies or any other problem, none of that. The ENT checks the condition of the vocal cords. The most frequent risks of this intervention are an attack of these vocal cords and the accidental disappearance of the parathyroid glands.

November 13 in the morning, I take a shower with a horrible product supposed to rid the body of all impurities. I then put on this beautiful blouse that removes the little dignity that remains to the patient. Buttocks well in the air, which caricature well the image of the hospital. I am not at my first intervention, four times the knees, once the ankle and appendectomy. I am sailing in known territory, which almost eliminates the apprehension that can be felt before going on the operating table.

Comes the time of premedication. This rather painful injection in the buttocks which makes me float. In a euphoric state, the stretcher bearers lead me into the basement of the hospital to join the operating room. This one is like all blocks, light blue and extremely cold. I see the reassuring image of Dr. Meyer and a team around him. It is in all serenity that I inject the anesthetic product by the catheter pressed on the top of my hand ...

I open my eyes and quickly recognize the familiar and reassuring environment of my room. I'm still in total blur but without any pain, I try to assess the situation and I quickly realize that I can swallow much more easily. So, I have removed this damn thyroid, I just feel the discomfort of a large bandage at the neck.

The anesthetic product still circulates in my veins and I go back to sleep several times. The comforting moment comes, I'll finally be able to eat something, it's also a sign that everything is fine. I call Jeannette to reassure her and tell her the progress of the operation.

The time comes for the visits, which the day of the surgery are more of a constraint than a comfort so much one longs to sleep. Yet, these familiar faces are reassuring and always well intentioned. The day goes on until the evening meal waited impatiently and finally a complete calm in the room to start the night.

The night nurse conducts her tour with the traditional hospital herbal tea. it is not especially good but still very comforting. I remember sneezing hard enough just then. Sneezing is already an earthquake in a healthy body, I thought at that moment that all the threads of the scar were torn off. The nurse lifted the bandage and checked, the stitches was in place.

It was during the night that things started to get complicated. I have more and more trouble breathing and swallowing. Things get pretty fast and I call the nurse at night, I never had to use this button before. It does not take long for her to arrive, I try to explain what happens but my voice is completely distorted, it is as if I spoke by making a gargle. She does not take long to call the duty doctor, I had never seen him before.

- *He has internal bleeding, he must go to the block urgently!*

Now I cannot speak anymore, the least sound comes out of my throat. I breathe harder and harder, when I'm in the elevator, I imagine myself breathing through the tube of a pen, completely stupid to think that at this moment. Each breath becomes more painful and less and less air fills my lungs, I do everything to save each puff, I do not move, I am a surprising calm. Any agitation would make the situation even more difficult.

I find myself again in the basement of the hospital, three people run down the hall pushing my bed. I see the neon scrolls above my head, I remember thinking about the TV series where we could see this kind of images, even more stupid to think that!

This corridor seems interminable, they run, the neon's continue to scroll like my thoughts. I feel the end close, I see it. I think of Jeannette alone in Shanghai who will panic when she learns of my death. To Anais my daughter who may not understand that I'm not here anymore. My last thought is very selfish for me: I will never be the woman I wanted to be, the woman who is in my genes, my biggest regret ...

Still in the hallways, I remember my last breath, I kept control until the end, no panic. This last breath, I think about it every day since this operation. I 'll never see the block, it's over, no way to get any molecule of air into my lungs. The eyes close ... I feel my heart now stop, it's over! I did not move, not panicked, nothing ...

I have read in testimonies of people in imminent death that we see his life scroll, a great white light waiting for us, I have not seen anything like it. I felt the end close, the images came in accelerated, it's true, but I did not feel anything else. The most frightening were the calm and serenity with which I lived this experience, I knew it was the end, I did not have the slightest fear or even apprehension about this inevitable death, I was ready!

When I open my eyes, there is only blue, pure blue and beautiful, so it is well finished and there is something after death. I do not know how long I fixed this beautiful light, a few seconds? several minutes? No idea.

Turning my head, I realize that I am connected to several places and probably find myself in the resuscitation room. My bed is next to the window and the weather outside is beautiful, it is the beautiful blue sky that I saw and here I am back down on earth, alive. When I realized my situation, I smiled and cried, I get a second chance, a second life.

After the morgue, resuscitation room is probably the worst place to be in the hospital. The highly qualified staff is technically the habit of treating vegetables, bodies almost lifeless and above all voiceless.

- *What does he want this one to ask me questions?*

I wanted to know, to try to understand what had happened. ICU is a place where the notion of time does not exist, you are not punctuated by meals, only infusions feed you, you are connected everywhere, no way to move or go to the bathroom ... you're a vegetable among the vegetables.

Dr. Meyer had been woken up in the middle of the night trying to get me back, he's the first to come to see me when I wake up.

- *You made us a joke, we had a hard time getting you back!!!*

The surgery had just ended because his green blouse was stained with blood, probably mine. I guess the pressure was such as opening the scar that all the blood had to come out at once.

There is relief at the announcement of the return to the room. Leave this sordid environment as soon as possible, a chance I stayed only a few hours.

I expected to see Jeannette going back to my room, but no, nobody. After what had happened to me, I imagined her jumping on the first plane! In any case, that's what I would have done, too bad, I would have appreciated her presence.

It is after a first meal and the removal of the urinary catheter that I really resume life in every sense of the word.

It is also the ballet of visits:

- *You made us a hell of fear, do not do it again!!!*

Exactly the kind of remarks you want to hear in those moments, you did all that just to bother them ... Without the least idea of what I was able to cross, I almost feel guilty, of course it is without any intention of harming.

I have no idea how Jeannette reacted when she heard what was going on. She just criticized for not having let her come with me ... as if I could have foreseen ...

Dr. Meyer is finally coming back to see me, this time wearing a clean white blouse, what a contrast compared to this morning. A small artery at the base of the neck had loosened, probably because of my sneezing, and the blood spilled into this cavity that had been stretched the day before. The pressure had become such that the trachea was completely blocked, no way to breathe. When I arrived at the block, I was in respiratory and cardiac arrest ...

- *You owe life to the anesthetist on duty, who is from the old school, he did not hesitate for a second to intubate you by force. If a young man had been on duty, the time that he plugs all the machines, you would not be alive.*

A chance in bad luck, such as staying alive or not is holding on to so little. When I see myself in a mirror, my neck is huge, a horror. The bottom of my mouth, my neck, my chest shows a purple blue color. The intubation has damaged all tissues but it is really a lesser evil. My ribs are also very painful, the one who gave me the heart massage went forcibly.

I recover slowly, the days are long and the nights distressing, the fear that it starts again is omnipresent. then from the exit visit, the doctor tells me:

- *I told you about the risk of hemorrhage, a case on 200,000! I wanted to thank you, you are My case ... I should now be quiet until retirement.*

This of course on the tone of the joke. It was really the fault of no luck, nobody can be held responsible for my troubles.

Not so simple, not easy to live without thyroid, lots of things are deregulated and it takes months to stabilize. Not easy either to leave after having lived his own death.

"One" gave me a second chance, I do not know who this is "One", Destiny, luck, a divine will, no idea. Still need to start this new life, we do not see all things in the same way, something changed, I changed.

My last thought before "dying" was to regret not having been able to live as a woman although genetically female. In this second life ... I will be a woman.

CHAPTER 8

I RETURN TO SHANGHAI to find Jeannette and resume the daily grind. This return is much more complicated than I had imagined. Extreme fatigue, dizziness and sometimes difficulty walking.

Jeannette cannot find better on my arrival than to blame me for the fear that I made her ... yet, knowing me in intensive care, she did not move from Shanghai! In short, I come back to life almost miraculously but with great difficulty in recovering. Living without a thyroid is much more serious than I thought. I really took it too lightly. The Levothyroxine replaces the missing gland, we start at 100mg and adjust according to blood tests every 3 weeks. As long as the TSH is not good, it is necessary to increase or possibly decrease the treatment in steps of 0.25mg. As my equilibrium rate is 250mg, it will take more than a year of trouble to finally find the right dosage.

The doctors thought that after the surgery, I would not have these problems of high blood pressure, it is not the case. I take 3 drugs which are supposed to adjust the blood pressure but they have very little effect, I am every day at 180/120 ... We do not really feel good with such a blood pressure!

Moreover, when one is in hypothyroidism, the weight gain is fast, which of course is my case. Nothing goes, health is not at the rendezvous, my character changes and not in a good way, Jeannette increasingly nostalgic for France. Her stays with me are shorter and shorter, there is always joy in the reunion, but the intensity drops continuously.

My work at the factory is going pretty well, the Americans are proposing several projects of expansions and investments, we have excellent relationship. The difference in mentality between the people of Minnesota and California surprises me, no comparison, when all sounds wrong in the south, the north seems so sincere.

Several times I traveled to St. Cloud, MN, USA, a city an hour away from Minneapolis, the state of a thousand lakes. The scenery is beautiful, the people are charming but the food is a disaster, double or triple portions compared to what we usually eat. Always full of sauce, ketchup or mayonnaise.

Despite my weight gain, in the United States I am considered lean, what weak consolation!

As much as the relations with the Americans are in good shape, so the relations with Robert, my former boss in France, deteriorate. After only three years of seniority, I become General Manager, our American bosses place us at the same level ... it does not pass, he has trouble accepting it. We were so close, we spent our holidays in Corsica together, we had great moments and then nothing. Of course, the distance does a lot but I feel a real rancor, a lot of unspoken feelings. Gerard keeps coming from time to time when I ask for his help, he perceives the same tension. He is much more relaxed, he feels happy to see his student in this position, exactly what he had planned.

It's been three years now that we live in China, I started to learn the language... To speak only, ideograms seem too complicated. Despite the four tones, the language is not as difficult to learn as it seems. Grammar is relatively simple; one can even find words just by association. For example, everything that is electric starts with Dian, a TV is Dian Shi (see), an elevator is Dian Ti (electric scale).

After a few months, I manage, I can negotiate, order at the restaurant or ask for directions. Let's say it's a basic survival Chinese but the natives are impressed and proud when a Laowai (foreigner) speaks their language, you get what you want ...

We are in 2010, the Shanghai World Expo will soon open. The embassy invites French nationals to participate to a cocktail party for the speech of our dear President Sarkozy. I do not like him at all, my ballot never leaned to the right. However, this is a great opportunity to have a drink at the expense of the republic. Sarko does not come alone, three full Airbus for a delegation, a real megalomania. The reception is held at 2 pm in one of the most beautiful hotels in the city, just on the Bund with a magnificent view of Pudong, the new city on the other side of the Yanpu River. Accompanied by a friend, we decide to have lunch at the hotel to avoid traffic jams. Sarko's star guest, Alain Delon plans to make an appearance, the Chinese are crazy, they know him all!

We reach the hotel at 11:30 AM, the restaurant is on the top floor. The door of the elevator opens, I recognize Rachid Kimoun, a talented sculptor, the husband of Eve Ruggieri (famous TV presenter) to whom he holds the arm. We spent some good evenings at the "Cork" restaurant, he came regularly to Shanghai. At next to them are Luc Chatel, Minister of Education, Xavier Bertrand, Minister of Labor, Laurence Parisot, CEO of the MEDEF (main employers' organization in France) and finally our dear Mr. Kouchner, Minister of Foreign Affairs.

- *Hi Rachid, how are you?*

I salute him and his wife without paying too much attention to the other politicians, though much more publicized. Mr. Kouchner takes offense and launches me:

- *Hello!*

A hello in my back in a very insistent and ironic tone, translate: "you did not recognize me silly? ". In a totally involuntary way, I touched a nerve, I'm happy to step on his toes, ... Having met him elsewhere, I have never met a person more narcissistic and pretentious than him.

Sarko's words sound so wrong, you wonder who writes his speeches for him. The following champagne flutes are much better...

Every weekend, I find my friends René, Bruno and Jean-Michel, we are the survivors, so many expatriates have left in the last two years. We almost always find ourselves at the same restaurant, we make the world around a Beaujolais. We usually end the evening at Manhattan, a famous Shanghai bar where girls from all over Asia come together to find the rich man they are waiting for. There is really everything, everything is allowed. One night, there was an Air France crew, half-naked girls on the stage and the pilot could not walk anymore because he was drunk. Fortunately, I did not take this flight the next day!

We are entitled every year to the month of free husband. This is a time when wives return to France for the summer holidays and their beloved husbands still have to work. The Chinese girls are very familiar with this period, it's time to catch a "westerner" and do everything to fall in love. Incredible success we have during these few weeks. None of us have fallen into this trap.

Unfortunately, all these beautiful things ended in one go. Paul, the boss of Stearns I depend on comes to eat at home and slipped a big envelope. Inside, I discovered the K2 Group stock options worth about $ 20,000. First time I'm directly concerned with stock options, I had just heard about it without really knowing.

Curiously, Paul apologizes for not being able to do better and I would understand later!

It took only a few days to learn that the K2 group which weighs $3 billion was bought by another group which weighs $5 billion!

And here we go from one hand to another by a simple signature. These big US investment funds have absolutely no respect for the human side of the business, they manipulate numbers, they govern everything. In one fell swoop, thousands of jobs disappear, 20 years, 30 years of seniority and experience, no importance. The only objective is to sell the companies two or three years later by a substantial margin.

As part of a buyout, stock options became shares that I converted into cash. I never agreed to make money with business gambling except by savings but not by speculation. My speech seems outdated, another generation? Only the value of labor should produce income, speculation is not part of it.

From a company in France where we were 20 people, I work in a group that has tens of thousands of employees all over the world! Just one more pawn on a planetary chessboard.

I now depend on Coleman, a large American company specializing in camping and owner of the Camping Gaz brand in France.

The head office is in Wichita, Kansas, the center of the United States, the world's asshole, my new boss is Bob... Nothing to do with the mentality of the north of the USA, these people are arrogant, America first and imagine the rest of the planet as negligible. All planned investments and projects are canceled. The Americans clearly want to avoid any potential scandal with factories in Asia. If for example, children worked in one of their factories, the share could collapse... It is better not to have a factory at all to avoid this kind of inconvenience. Children, we do not care, shareholders are much more important than any of the employees.

Very quickly, Stearns in the USA is dismantled, my previous boss is fired in the American way, "you leave on the field" and escorted to the exit ... what a despicable way to proceed, you give everything you have to run a company and we throw you out like a mess?

Happy French employees who have a labor contract, paid leaves, a notice in case of dismissal, severances, unemployment benefits... The United States is the world's leading power? Yes, but at what price? None of this exists!

Sevylor in France is next on the list, all my former colleagues including Robert are fired. Fortunately, they are French with notice and compensation. My contract is transferred to Camping Gaz in the Lyon region.

The Shanghai factory is next on the list.

CHAPTER 9

COLEMAN WILL MAKE THEIR DECISION SHORTLY, I know that the Shanghai factory will disappear. I'm waiting for the penalty to fall, but we still have to continue producing, difficult to find any motivation.

The morale is low, I will soon lose my job, I no longer pay attention to me, the pounds accumulate, I smoke a lot and I drink more than reason.

I will never be a woman and it gnaws me, I always complain to Jeannette.

- *Rather than complaining, try to do something for others if you cannot do it for you!*

A good slap, one more, as if the situation was not already complicated. Thinking about it, she's right, what could I do?

A few years ago, I contacted ABC association that offers a framework to people who like me suffer from gender dysphoria, I make an appointment with Sandra who works as a volunteer at the railway museum in Mulhouse. When I arrive, I ask to the guy at the entrance to talk to Sandra as we have an appointment:

- *There is no Sandra working here!*
- *Yet I was given an appointment here.*
- *Ahhh, you probably want to talk about Paul?*

What a horror of being called so while Sandra lives fully as a woman, poor guy! She tells me about the association, the different members and invites me to participate in an evening in a hotel restaurant in the area. I tremble at the thought of appearing in public dressed as a woman. D-Day, Jeannette advises me on how to dress, she would like to come with me ... more to watch me than for anything else. I arrive at the restaurant dressed as a man, several girls are already there, I share the aperitif and then I go to a room to get dressed and make up. I have a panic fear, what am I doing here? I go out at last, we are served the meal, the server calls us ma'am knowing very well who we are, all that sounds wrong, so wrong, it's not for me!

I realize that I am not in my place, to disguise myself in front of everyone annoys me to the highest point. I cannot imagine going for a walk with these people under the mocking glances of passers-by. No, I'm not like them, I will not attend their next meetings.

I'm always looking for a solution, what could I do to finally feel a little better, feel myself? With my skills in website creation, I start the development of an e-commerce website. It will market all that is necessary for a man who like me wants to be a woman or likes to cross-dress. I deposit my domain name which will be www.enfemmeshop.com

I use Prestashop, an open source software that allows you to access the code and program yourself. The website looks good, very professional looking, management of the quantities available, secure payment, choice of mode of delivery, I'm happy, I spent nights and weekends. The activity starts slowly, I put only a few references to test and manage supplies. I recruited my assistant at the Shanghai factory that handles all purchases in China, I create an offshore company in Hong Kong for trading between China and France.

From one to two orders per week, we go to one per day, then five per day, then ten ... We must quickly create a microbusiness to declare all these revenues. The most requested items are the fake silicone breasts, circles, triangles, water drop shapes, all diameters, all sizes ... The other flagship products are shoes with heels up to 45 (11 US size), wigs, underwear and dresses.

On the professional side, as I would have expected, Coleman asks me to prepare a plan to fire everyone and close the factory.

I cannot do it, there must be another solution. I contact several professional connections that may be interested in a recovery but without success. I then go back to the former owner Michael Lee, the one who sold to the Americans. I really played on his sensitivity: everything he created will be dismantled, all these workers he knows for years will disperse, all these skills get lost ... Bingo, he agrees to take over the factory. This is of course a good benefit for Coleman who did not expect so much.

I negotiate with them the value of repurchase and the conditions of dismissal because all employment contracts will have to be canceled. I gather all 650 employees in the canteen, a huge hubbub, rumors circulate, I must immediately extinguish the fire. I ask them to listen carefully to what I am going to tell them and not to react, wait for me to finish. I speak English, my Chinese is not enough for explaining something so important:

- *I have to tell you that Coleman decided to close the plant and they asked me to take care of it. I convinced Michael Lee to take over the factory. At the end of the month, you will all be fired, you will receive four months of severance and you are all rehired on the same day in the new company.*

To announce bad news when you're the boss is part of the work but then ... I was entitled to a standing ovation, it deeply moved me. I do not know how many bosses were applauded this way after announcing a complete collective dismissal! I am proud and really happy for everyone, we could not hope better.

Now remains the negotiation of my dismissal! My French colleagues were dismissed based on French law, I report to Americans. They offer me a compensation of 120,000 €, I could pretend to € 10,000 if I had remained in France!!!

- *Do you want to negotiate or the amount is fine for you?*

Obviously, such a sum is perfect for me especially as the transfer agreement, I will continue to receive my income during 6 months for "transfer of jurisdiction". I sign the agreement with a smile hard to veil ... Until I find one of their internal documents: they had planned a maximum of $ 400,000 for my dismissal, but what an idiot, so stupid to not negotiated even a minute!!!

Well, you still have to understand, I'll receive 12 times what I would have gotten in France, I have to satisfy myself.

The transition is going well, the Americans have honored their commitments, all the allowances have been paid.

As far as I'm concerned, I went to Lyon in this Camping-Gaz company that pays me for several months, first time for me to go there. I met the HR manager, I sign all documents and get this valuable check ... I have never had a 6-digit amount ... not even in francs. During the 2-hour journey that separates Lyon from my home in Alsace, I look at it several times and of course go directly to the bank.

Once at the counter, I ask to deposit a check:

- *For check deposits, go through the deposit machine next to the ATM*
- *Sorry, but this check will not go into the machine*

Seeing the amount, she did not insist ... see our checking account with more than 120,000 € after so many galleys in the past ... it feels good. We want to call his banker 10 times a day to ask him the balance on the account ... They love it!

The six months of transfer of competence passed quickly, Michael asked me to return to France to create a company that will distribute the inflatable and fitness products (another activity he has) in Europe.

China is finished, I'm not disappointed to leave, so tired by the attitude of the Chinese. Money has everything perverted, everything is due, the other has no importance and everything is good to earn more.

The driving in Shanghai becomes extremely painful, I passed my license to gain independence. The rule is the law of the strongest, everything is allowed, it is stressful. I arrive at work exhausted nervously, and in the evening, I arrive home angry.

Be aware that the French embassy urged us never to intervene or rescue the wounded in an accident. These rescued file complaints against the rescuer under the pretext of having aggravated his case. Chinese justice is very simple: in a conflict between a Chinese and a foreigner, the Chinese always win whatever the cause. When this happens, these unfortunate rescuers will pay astronomical sums and there is no question of leaving the country until everything is settled.

The return to France is not so easy, it is necessary to get used to another rhythm, another climate, another food. In addition, the sales job is really not what I like to do, I always seem to rob the customer asking him to pay ... The company is created, I manage the flow of goods and prospects to some potential customers.

Robert, my former boss, got wind of my return and my new activity. He was quick to contact Michael Lee, highlighting his formidable skills to sell and insisting of course on my weaknesses. Robert is undoubtedly more proficient than me but I really did not expect to get shot in this way.

The EnFemmeShop website is more and more successful, the revenues become substantial but we need more space, we manage all the stock and orders from our cellar ... Every day, we deposit 10 to 20 parcels at the post office and in a relay point.

We have a disused barn right next to our house, this would be the perfect place: not only would we put the barn in value but above all, we would be on site. The work starts quickly, only the half-timbered structure is preserved, all the rest is redone: the roof, the walls, the floors... everything! I make the plans with the eventual idea of converting this barn into an apartment if the activity ceases.

The new premises are beautiful, the shelves are quickly installed and all the stock is in place. I use Google Ads for optimal positioning based on keywords, we quickly move to 6,000 customers. 6,000 people who for the most part are hiding to have these few moments of happiness, how many hundreds of lives have been shattered just because of the look of society? The company's sales contact is Céline, she answers all emails, sends promotions and signs documents. A semblance of existence for Céline ...

A year after starting the company of Michael Lee, he comes to France and announces my dismissal. Thank you, Robert! Curiously, it is him who resumed the activity, probably a good revenge for him!

Well, what to do now? China, I have already given, work in France for not even half salary is not motivating either.

Exploiting the website would be a solution but working with Jeannette every day without leaving the house seems beyond my strength. In addition, I miss Asia, if one is stung, it acts like a virus.

One of the clients I proposed to sell the plant to is Japanese, Takashina, the American branch is made up of my former colleagues from Stearns. For a year, Simon Takashina, the vice president who also lived in Shanghai had invited me regularly to offer me to work for them what I had always refused. Perhaps it would be time to look at this proposal more closely?

The job will be to run a factory in Hanoi which is in great financial difficulty ...

First, I sign a three-month evaluation mission, including two months at the factory. For the first time, I land in Vietnam, a new country to add to the list. Simon, the current General

Director of the factory, is waiting for me there. My hotel room is in the city center, right next to an imposing cathedral. I find the sound of bells so usual in France. Simon makes me discover my first Vietnamese meals, it's just excellent, I did not expect such quality. I'm right in the middle of the historic center of Hanoi, the 36 streets each with a specialty: Silk Street, Tinsmith Street, Musical Instruments Street ... A real anthill, thousands of scooters everywhere who use their horns all the time, drivers crazier than each other. Incredible, I am in the middle ages, a real anarchy on the road. I thought frankly that after having driven in Shanghai, I will be able to roll everywhere ... I was wrong.

I discover a new culture, the Vietnamese are so different from the Chinese. They have a smile culture like the Thai. I visit the war museum, I learn a lot about the French occupation and the war lost, all seen the Vietnamese side of course, speaking of French imperialists. This colonial time when the premises were considered as less than nothing by French, all powerful. The reaction of the Vietnamese on this subject is quite confusing: "the French built everything, the Americans destroyed everything but we never lost a war. It is true that many magnificent buildings, hospitals, water towers, the prison date from the French presence. Vietnamese do not feel the slightest rancor, it's past.

The Red River plant looks like nothing, a total disorganization, a Vietnamese Canadian person controls the production, another Bulgarian person runs the administration but they do not communicate. A real war where some Vietnamese make their law by intimidation. By doing a detailed analysis of the costs of production, I quickly realize drifts and many suspicious figures, it seems that we pay some suppliers much more than it should. In addition, a lot of cash disappears without any justification.

I get the most documents, this month has passed so quickly. I'm not appreciated by some, I just put my nose in their tricks and of course, they do not like that. I go back to France, I have one month to peel all the documents and make an initial assessment.

I make a trip again in November 2011 to finalize the report and try to find evidences of what I had discovered. No supplier or subcontractor confesses to paying retro commissions to some managers, we must find another way, they will not bite the hand of those who feed them. I decide to make an appointment at a reputable law firm to evaluate the different possibilities. This information has circulated very quickly, the way to achieve it is simple: it is enough that the driver knows it. A driver is worse than a janitor, you always have that in mind.

The lawyer explains to me that paying commissions is done in all the companies in Vietnam, it's almost something normal. In any case, the whole system is corrupt, including the police and justice. However, I discovered that most providers use fake invoices to avoid paying taxes I understand that violating the laws does not scare them at all, however, dealing with the tax is a different story, they are terrified when it touches their wallet, it is on this that I'm going to trap them. I do not know who to trust in the factory, my strategy is simple: I speak of my discovery left and right. It did not drag on, three days later, these same suppliers ask to see me and suddenly become very talkative. I record all conversations, the evidence is overwhelming, a small group of people, including the Vice General Director, recover considerable sums. The five of them, they would have diverted more than a million dollars in three years, incredible that nobody has ever seen anything!

My report is ready and armored, I have to present it to the shareholders, they will decide if they want me to run the factory.

The shareholders are stunned by my discoveries and amounts misappropriated, they are angry against themselves to have let the situation rot for 3 years.

Unsurprisingly, they offer me the position of General Manager with the mission to restore the factory in the next three years.

Bingo, I have my contract in hand, a good salary and very good benefits such as travel, housing and insurance. I accept on the condition that they approve my management method while promising them quick results ...

I impose another condition I do travel in business class. After all, they came to pick me up, I can afford some requirements.

When I take the reins of the factory, the situation is catastrophic. Some managers graciously use the cash register and touch commissions from different suppliers. In three years, the book loss is close to $ 1.8 million for a plant that has barely 180 employees.

To profit personally from the company's money is for me just inadmissible. My first job is to clean up the gangrenous parts. Firing someone is never easy, but when it comes to people who have diverted the money from the company to the detriment of the workers ... it's relatively easy! I'm crazy, I must pay severances that they take with a wide ironic smile, I have only contempt for these people, I just want to stick them to the wall! Impossible to start legal proceedings even if the evidence is overwhelming.

After this big broom, I could win the confidence of the team in place. The factory starts to work properly. After one year, we make the first profits. I insist on the shareholders so that a part of the profit is distributed to all the staff. I want to prevent this commission system from starting again and the best way is to share it with everyone. I was very clear with all the staff, anyone who will benefit from personal financial benefits to the detriment of the company, be it subcontractors or suppliers, will be fired on the spot without any compensation. It may not be legal but they will not go to court either.

Wages are neither higher nor lower than elsewhere but everyone is respected, Vietnamese social law is applied to the letter, which is really not common here. My role is primarily to ensure that each team can work and communicate together.

Dad, you're so beautiful

CHAPTER 10

BANGKOK, ONE DAY TO D-DAY BEFORE THE SURGERY. Alone in my hotel room, I go around in circles. I go from euphoria to anxiety constantly, damn, the night is going to be long.

I had a good cocktail at the bar, a Mai Tai, my favorite, probably my last drink as a man. This evening and the morning of tomorrow will be full of "last times". A light meal quickly swallowed, I need to be alone, to think about my new life and enjoy these moments. It is the last meal of the condemned, condemned at last to be happy, that the punishment is beautiful!

I have to drink a product that according to Boun is simply disgusting. It is imperative to empty these 3 bottles to wash my intestines. 3 shots spaced 30 minutes, the first small bottle is swallowed, it's not so terrible, it's frankly disgusting but bearable. Mistake, the taste in the mouth is just awful and persists even drinking several glasses of water and we will have to repeat it again twice ...

It was with the greatest difficulty and a lot of disgusting that I carry out this repugnant step. As expected, a good part of the evening is spent in the bathroom.

Lying, the light on, sleep does not come, a smug smile floods my face. My suitcase is ready, I must leave at 6 am tomorrow morning for the Piyavate hospital. Of course, no breakfast, no drinks or food after midnight.

The night was very short but without the least anxiety. I check out, the driver is already there waiting for me. This is not the cart for the guillotine but that the road seems so long. 20 minutes separate us from the hospital, they seem to have lengthened them during the night.

Only emergencies are open, I am expected, I am given a bracelet, I become a barcode that will be scanned at each intervention. A quick blood test then a nurse leads me to what will be my room. Room 1020 on the 10th floor will remain etched forever in my memory.

The door opens ... hospital rooms, I've known but this one is the one I was waiting for. It is spacious, the bed seems comfortable, a small lounge, a fridge and a bathroom. Well folded on the bed, which I imagine to be the famous hospital gown. The nurse shows me where to put the suitcase and asks me to put on this famous piece of fabric so characteristic, which I do.

What a surprise, finally a blouse that does not reduce the patient to a piece of meat leaving the buttocks visible to everyone. The blouse is worn, you are no longer a person, you are an illness, a room number or a character trait.

This new blouse I wear is not at all like that, it is almost elegant and respects the dignity of the person. Another nurse arrives with a care cart, ... time for a shave!

I lie down, she goes back my blouse and oh surprise, the work is already done. Just before leaving Hanoi, I asked Linh, my favorite masseuse, to do a complete waxing of the bikini ...

What a funny word to define this area of the human body. She did not have the right to do that on a man but she knows the reason and supports me from the beginning. She broke the rules and did the housework. When handling sex, there was not the least reaction or even the slightest sensation, it's just an inert piece of meat that would disappear ... I discovered for the first time the joys of bikini waxing!

I never had a problem wearing this sex, I used and abused it, it did its job but it is really time to move on.

The nurse seems happy to have nothing to do, she asks me to take a shower with an antiseptic product. It's more like a classic shower gel, so different from traditional betadine. Really, France would have a lot to learn!

My departure to the block is scheduled at 10am, two hours to wait. I sit in my bed and against all odds, I fall asleep.

When I wake up, three people are busy around my bed, it's time, we go down. Quick, one last pee, my LAST standing pee in front of the toilet. Usually, there is always a fear, a ball in the stomach when the time to lie on the surgery table arrives. Today, it is not so, I am so calm, happy. How can we be happy to spend hours on a hard table like stone to be under the knife? Well, it exists, I live it at this moment. I will not undergo surgery, I will benefit, it represents a huge difference.

My bed moves, two stretcher bearers push it, the elevator then 10 floors down, my bed circulates under the neon lights. I cannot help but think of my internal bleeding after thyroid removal.

Today is very different, I chose to be there, I realize my dearest wish. The door opens on an area that must certainly include several operating rooms. An anthill of multicolored blouses, each having a distinct function. Everyone seems to come out of the same mold, the head covering and the mask make all this population anonymous ... Here I am in "my" block. I move from the bed to the operating table, my god it's so cold, it's cold in all blocks, there is usually the smell of death but not today.

The IV line on the top of my hand is placed, the plastic pipes mix and immediately diffuse their liquid. They install the cuff for blood pressure, the sensors for the heart, the machine on my left begins to emit its characteristic beep-beeps. I recognize the anesthetist who speaks good English. All around me, people are busy, talking, laughing. The gestures are safe, no room for improvisation, I count 24 people in the room and the surgeons are not there yet ... So many people to take care of me.

The armband squeezes and relaxes:

- *Well, you're not stressed Céline*

What a beautiful "Celine", the meter displays 110/80 and 58 beats per minute, difficult to be calmer. I'm good, so good, I know that nothing can stand in the way of my deepest desire.

My head is tilted back, I see the two surgeons returning. My legs are put in gynecological position, it is 10:20am.

- *We'll go, I put the mask on you and you count to 10.*

From experience, I know we never get to 5, we sleep before. The mask is applied to my face, I remember winking at the anesthetist. I sleep!

CHAPTER 11

SEPTEMBER 2011, HANOI HAS NOTHING TO DO WITH SHANGHAI, it seems that 30 years of evolution separate them... I often compare the two and I find it hard to find my place. The streets are full of motorcycles loaded to the extreme, sidewalks, when they exist, are used by these motorcycles, you have to walk on the road and constantly avoid passing vehicles. It's the jungle, everyone sees themselves as a priority and the horn serves as proof.

What am I doing here? I will never hold on! The few sidewalk spaces available are used by street restaurants, the women come with their handrails, the baskets, filled with a side of mini-stools and the other, everything necessary to prepare a meal. We settle on these tiny chairs and enjoy these different preparations. I must admit that you eat very well and for only a few cents. Vietnamese cuisine reconciles me with my presence here. These smells of spices at every street corner, mini barbecues with the typical Asian smell, humm!

The city center is filled with tourists, the perfect place to discover the city but certainly not to live there. I contact a real estate agent advised by the French community. After several visits, I choose a brand-new apartment on a kind of island overlooking Truc Bach lake. It has two bedrooms, a very large living room, dining room and kitchen. The apartment is furnished but all closets are empty. I fill two caddies at the supermarket, it is absolutely necessary to buy everything: plates, glasses, pots, a broom, sheets, everything ... The first days are like camping but I'm at home, it's always better than staying at the hotel.

Only a small bridge where two cars can just cross allow access to this island. One night, I find myself stuck on this bridge with a big limousine that brushes us, we cannot move. Hundreds of people are screaming behind this car, but what's that shit? I chose this place to be quiet and now hundreds of hysterical Vietnamese follow this car. We are side by side, the cars are brushing against each other, a window in the back of the car opens, his head tells me something. With the shouting and the music, I hear, I realize that it's the Korean who sings Gangnam style... I open my window, we meet face to face and we shake hands... That doesn't affect me one way, but what did he come here to do in this backwater in Hanoi? Finally, police channels this hysterical crowd and I can go home.

Jeannette discovers Hanoi for the first time, she has no problem of adaptation but she does not settle as when we were expatriated to China. She will only stay there for a few weeks; the grandchildren and her daughter miss her as she sets foot away from home. Her home is already no longer with me, her home is in France, far from me.

The management of EnFemmeShop continues to grow, I hired Patricia, Jeannette's best friend, to take care of the deliveries, to unload and allow Jeannette to spend more time with me. But she has gotten into the game of this new activity and is keen to control orders and deliveries. In my presence, she spends most of her time on the computer giving instructions to Patricia. A convenient excuse to shorten her presence with me, she considers herself essential to the operation of the company.

Having exceeded the maximum sales amount for self-entrepreneurs during two years in a row, it is mandatory to switch into a formal company, I form a joint-stock company. Taxes are much higher and incomes fall drastically. We must work even harder, invest in advertising and develop new applications. A second day of work after the factory, it starts to become wearisome, especially as Jeannette does the same ... All that for money! What a mistake to go into company, I should have just voluntarily limited my turnovers and stayed a self-entrepreneur!

After a few months in my apartment, I begin to get depressed, the sewers pour into the lake just in front, the smell is atrocious, there is nothing around, no restaurants, no shops, it forces me to move. In addition, a building is under construction next door, they have the good idea to pour the concrete at night and use a very powerful vibrator. Everything shakes in the middle of a noise that prevents any possibility of finding sleep. Moreover, living in an apartment stresses me. I have my scooter that allows me to move but they are so crazy on the road that I prefer to use it as little as possible.

I would like to move into a villa, have a pool, I talk to the shareholders, they do not discuss and just accept my request. Swimming is the only activity I can still practice with my damaged knees.

The houses with a pool are more like castles, they are huge, some have 10 rooms with bathroom, everything is too big. Finally, I find a smaller house, there are "only" 6 bedrooms and 6 bathrooms and a swimming pool of 10 meters sheltered. On the ground floor, the outdoor pool, a bar, a garden, a toilet and a shower for the pool. Pillars support the other 4 floors, 540 m^2 living space in total. I propose to the shareholders to enjoy the rooms rather than going to the hotel. Everyone is happy with this choice at $3,000 a month, my house becomes the Palace.

I feel good in this house, several palm trees in the garden provide an exotic appearance, the architecture is a copy of the old colonial houses, with very large columns. I enjoy my pool protected from all eyes, I can swim in a bikini in peace. In one of the large rooms, I install a golf simulator. It allows me to play as on a real course, an electronic system defines the trajectory of the ball. The balls finish their races on a huge canvas screen where are projected images of the course. The speed of some balls exceeds 200km/h, the noise of the impacts is rather impressive. I can play from home and with air conditioning. Playing on a golf course when the temperature exceeds 35° and a humidity rate close to 100% is a horror.

Despite the pool and my golf, I'm alone, I'm tired, I smoke, I drink too much, I spend my evenings programing. My scale shows more than 105kg, my image in the mirror disgusts me. During my last trip to France, my doctor diagnosed me with the onset of diabetes, I must start a treatment. By adding hypertension that becomes really problematic, the ankylosing spondylitis, the thyroid, the knees, alcohol and tobacco ... Too much is too much, for the second time in my life, I think of suicide in a serious way, it would settle everything! I only foresee two solutions: either I continue to let go which will lead me to an anticipated death, or I react immediately. But why react? I know I will never be a woman!

And then NO, FUCK THAT, I was entitled to a second life, a second chance, I do not have the right to spoil it, I must react.

We are on April 1st, 2015, from this date, I do not drink a drop of alcohol, I change my eating habits by switching to Vietnamese cuisine and I resume a daily physical activity by swimming an hour every day. That same April 1st, I start my hormonal treatment with estrogen and anti-androgens.

Especially not to take example on this self-medication, this method is to be absolutely prohibited. But in Vietnam, the possibility of meeting an endocrinologist who will prescribe appropriate treatment is non-existent. The pharmacies look like grocery stores, you go in with your shopping list, you do not have to worry about getting the drugs at a ridiculous price. The only difficulty is finding a pharmacy that does not sell fake medicines from China.

To avoid doing anything wrong, I take an appointment with a French doctor practicing in a nearby clinic, I explain my approach by email before meeting him. Hervé is not comfortable with my approach, it shows. He remains very professional in his attitude. Anyway, I'm not looking for his approval, just a follow-up. Every two months, I will take a blood test to check the different levels of hormones.

In parallel, I take an appointment with a French psychologist who practices in another clinic. Me who had sworn never to see a shrink ... Like what, never say never.

My approach is voluntary, I feel that I need a crutch or at least a mirror, I must at all costs keep my feet on the ground and not do anything wrong, do not get carried away.

I have all the attention of Laetitia, she does not judge, does not speak of disease and immediately speaks to me feminine... what a slap and what a joy... Finally, someone to talk to ... We'll meet each week. She did an amazing job, I owe her a lot.

3 months after my strong decision, the scale shows 12 kilos less, I still do not drink alcohol, hypertension has completely disappeared, all the symptoms have disappeared, it is the same for diabetes.

With Laetitia, lots of doors open, she puts words on so many feelings, frustrations, everything becomes so simple.

Because of the hormones and my genetic inheritance, my breasts develop very quickly, they evolve exactly like those of a teenager, they become more and more visible.

I have the impression of arriving at a point of no return, there is still time to stop everything, otherwise it is necessary to move up a gear, to take new steps. I make an appointment with a speech therapist who practices in the same clinic as Laetitia. Tiphaine is surprised, she never had this kind of request but obviously, it is a challenge that interests her. I could have vocal cords surgery but it's a Russian roulette, it can succeed as it can completely fail, I prefer to play the safety card even if a lot of work will be needed.

Finally, I start laser facial hair removal sessions in a small spa, there are not many machines available on Hanoi. My hair, especially the legs and torso made me look like a bear. With the taking of hormones, everything is gone except facial hair that unfortunately are not affected.

Every Friday, I see my psychiatrist, my speech therapist and laser treatment. With Tiphaine, the job is to relearn how to breathe, everything must come from the belly, the work is effective but long, so long. She likes to say that the voice is the reflection of the soul, it's so true. The men have a voice frequency between 80 and 160 hertz, the voice of the women varies between 180 and 250 hertz. I have a deep voice, around

100 Hz, it will take months to double this frequency to obtain a natural voice. What does a man of this age do with a speech therapist who mainly receives children?

I combine all this work with the EnFemmeShop website and Jeannette who complains more and more. I am tired of all this, additional work but especially the attitude of my wife. I ask my accountant to proceed to a cessation of activity, it is better to stop before it degenerates especially as there is no debt. This site is my baby, it is really death in the soul that I ask for this cessation. It was also a mission, I understand exactly the request of these thousands of men and I answered. But here we have to make choices, despite the additional workload, incomes are becoming leaner. I hope this will have the effect of bringing Jeannette back a little more often to Hanoi.

The discussions with Laetitia become more and more enriching, Jeannette sees many changes that worry her.

Although she was legitimately angry when I told her that I had started hormone therapy, she knows that a new step had been taken.

However, she supports me by saying:

- *Whatever you do or decide, I will follow you.*

What comforting words, it is sure that this step should not leave her on the side of the road. But this road, I really want to take it with her, I have always been a woman with her, I just want to live with the body that suits me. I will always be the same person, just happy to be able to live in accordance with my real gender. At this point in my transition, I do not think of any surgery at all, I'm just happy that my body is changing.

She accompanies me to some consultations with Laetitia who shakes her a little:

- *It sucks, you pay a shrink so she tells you what you want to hear.*

In fact, Laetitia tells her things she does not want to hear. Jeannette is scared, I understand her very well, Laetitia tells her:

- *Since the beginning of your relationship, you live with a woman, you know it, you accepted it, why does this pose a problem today?*

She cries, she probably thought that I would remain confined to a life of lies and crossdressing. By initiating this process of hormonal therapy, I did not think about reassignment surgery. This treatment allowed me to come out of a deep malaise. On the other hand, for Jeannette and for my doctor, I take these hormones just to get breasts. Ridiculous!

When you know the impact of such treatment, physical changes, fats moving, hair falling, breasts that grow, the character that changes, the libido that falls to zero accompanied by total helplessness. No, it's not "to get breasts". What I have between my legs is only used to urinate. I took some Viagra's and other magic pills at first to satisfy Jeannette but over time, it does not work anymore.

At the end of 18 months, I lost 20 kg, from 105kg I moved to 85kg, I set a new goal at 78kg, when I reach that weight, I will stop smoking.

My breasts are now C cup, I cannot hide them especially under a T-shirt. During a meeting at the factory, I explain to my managers that I am genetically a woman and that I had to take a drug that developed me breasts. I did not lie, I just did not say everything ... I reassure myself that way. Hang and Hieu, my two Vietnamese friends have already made me think that in Asia, it is not acceptable to see the nipples point through the fabric. All Asian bra are armored, nothing is likely to get through. Well, I am a man, nobody will tell me anything but it becomes difficult to manage.

I read everything about hormonal treatments and their effects, all the steps are familiar to me, I have no surprise except this pair of breasts that makes me so proud. Transgender people taking similar treatment usually get a A or B cup but not more. I can consider myself happy, I finally talk about me in the feminine.

For years, I wore bra with absolutely nothing to support, what a pleasure to finally see them doing their work. I always have the same pleasure to put it on in the morning but I discover the pleasure of removing it after a day of work. Between wearing it for two or three hours in the evening or a whole day, the difference is substantial.

Jeannette has more and more difficulties managing this situation, she is convinced that I see someone else, my desire for her being no longer the same. I can explain that on the one hand, the machinery does not work anymore and that on the other hand my libido is non-existent, she is convinced of the opposite. Relationships are becoming more and more tense, her absences are now constant, we spent three months together in the last year.

In October 2016, Michel and Martine spend a few days in Hanoi. They are the parents of Jeremy, a young man we have known for a long time, he is in a gay relationship with

Vincent. Both are very friends with Caroline, Jeannette's daughter.

We know each other but we're not close, yet we get along well. Both in their sixties, she is a pharmacist, he is electrician in a company in Switzerland. Martine is not blind, my breasts deform my T-shirt and she sees the drugs I take. For the first time, I felt comfortable enough to discuss, share my needs to talk about my hormonal treatment and all inherent difficulties.

They are very open-minded, we discuss my situation at random. Jeannette is also happy to be able to talk to someone else.

I dress as I wish at home, this is the first time that "strangers" see me. My face is not feminine but I feel good, I feel like a woman. During an evening, Martine tells me:

- *But you cannot go on living like that, you have to do something!*

Why did it take me this to click? What she said seemed obvious but I remained completely passive.

By their sincerity and the wonderful discussions we had, they are the spark that I needed. I owe a lot to both of them, I sincerely hope that there will be other magical moments like this one. The holidays are over, everyone goes back to France, including Jeannette.

Following the cessation of business, the renovated barn is now empty, we decide to make an apartment for rent. Finally, we change direction to make a B&B, a new way for Jeannette to stay in France, big mistake. The grandchildren miss her just like her daughter, the cord has never been cut, I am the one who prevents them from seeing each other, I become the enemy.

The cottage is beautiful, it is furnished and decorated with great taste, I love doing that. Once again, I see very well the finished housing, it is necessary to brave new colors, furniture then the result is bluffing.

Very quickly, we get a 4-star rating, the cottage includes a terrace, a private heated pool, a very large garden, sun loungers and all the comfort that can be expected inside.

I register the cottage on AirBnb and Booking. In 3 weeks, six months of booking are confirmed, a great success. Obviously, Jeannette cares to welcome guests, advise, she's really talented. I take care of the computer part, reservations, management of the advertisers and all the communication with the hosts.

She hardly ever comes to Hanoi, there is always another reason. Our next meeting is scheduled in Koh Samui in March 2017, a beautiful island in the Gulf of Thailand. I'm overwhelmed with work at the factory, I'll be away for a day or two. This is school holidays and Caroline will be there with the children, the only reason for Jeannette's presence. My daughter Anaïs is part of the trip, the two grandchildren and their father Nicolas. Add Jeremy, Vincent and the parents of Jeremy, Martine and Michel ... what a band!

I rented a bungalow with two rooms that is directly on the beach, the resort is huge and very well arranged. For the first time in my life, I'm on the beach wearing a bikini. The children are still sleeping, Jeannette is with me, we are both lying on a deckchair. Martine comes to join us. This swimsuit, I use it almost every day at home away from all eyes, this is the first time it sees the sun. A big hat, my detached hair, sunglasses, the illusion is perfect. Walkers pass near me, no one pays any attention, I go unnoticed, what a magical moment. Martine takes a picture of me and Jeannette, I had to immortalize this moment. These two women over the age of sixty have nothing to envy of the small babes circulating. They are beautiful women, I would really like to be as bad as them at their age. For the first time, I feel fulfilled, I am a woman among women. However, I stay most often lying, as soon as I get up, it is very difficult to hide this protuberance in my swimsuit. I still enjoy my first swim in a bikini, there are no words to describe these moments. Jeannette can see and understand my happiness, she understood that a page has been turned, that's exactly what I want to live on a daily basis.

The holidays over, everyone goes home, I'm alone again in Hanoi.

Martine sends me an email with a link to a documentary about a woman who made her transition, her name is Olivia Chaumont.

I did not watch this program, I drank it, I devoured it, I cried ... what a woman, what courage and we have so much in common. She made her transition at my age, she is just like me in Freemasonry, she is an architect, I was an architect of the internet.

She speaks of a wave that was stronger than the others and that was at the origin of the sex change. Olivia is my wave, there are no other paths, anyway, I cannot continue to take anti-androgens for life, it is absolutely necessary to do something, my decision is made, I must absolutely go through the surgery to finally reveal the person that I am really.

All my spare time is devoted to internet research, reading testimonials, evaluating the reputation of different surgeons ... 50,000 men and women come to Thailand each year for surgery related to gender change ... 50,000, this represents a significant number of surgeons. The list is long but quickly, a platoon of five or six stands out, the stars of the scalpel. Of course, the prices are accordingly. What an inestimable luxury not to be limited by these substantial fees.

To have one's operation is one thing, to live properly afterwards is another. I absolutely want to secure the professional aspect, have a guaranteed income, do not tell me "we'll see later". What is the point of living in harmony with one's gender if it is to find oneself completely destitute, without work and without a future?

I plan to work five more years, save enough money aside for early retirement and finally get surgery. I talk to Jeannette who provides lip service, five years is far, she has time to see and hope that I change my mind by then.

Gordon, one of the factory customers, is the first I talk to. Sitting at the table of a Japanese restaurant, I explain my project by going straight to the point. I am surprised to see how easy words come out and especially without feeling the least embarrassment, Laetitia has really done a great job.

Gordon is obviously surprised, these first words while raising his glass are:

- *Congratulations, of course you have to do it.*

Oops, I did not expect it, tears come, grrr. I never have imagined that it is so easy to talk about it and that it can be welcomed as easily.

Julien, my French colleague, is next, how is he going to take this news? Well, everything is exactly the same as with Gordon ... Amazing!

Andy, the English shareholder, has become a friend over the course of his visits. He always comes to sleep at the Palace, that's the name they gave to my house. It usually stays there for five to six days. This time, I have to tell him about it, it's him *who gives me the opportunity:*

- *I have an announcement to make to you, I will soon be grandfather.*

I know his three daughters, they spent a few days with him in Vietnam, two of them are pregnant.

- *I too have an announcement to make you.*

My speech is now comfortable, I unpack my whole story by finishing with the goal that I would like to achieve, just to be a woman. After the surprise, he asks me questions, congratulates me. We talk about this for an hour, at no time does he mentioned my position at the plant and the impact it could have...

I talked to five people, all took it extremely positively as something normal, how to anticipate such reactions?

It is at this precise moment that everything changes: but why wait five years? If everyone gets it so well, why waste time? So many things could happen in 5 years! Of course, Jeannette is not pleased with my reasoning and all the arguments are good to change my mind.

The last one I need to talk to secure my work is my Japanese boss, Yoshi, the most important of all. We will soon have a meeting of directors in Miyazaki in Japan, we change place for each meeting: Hanoi, Shanghai, Osaka, Tokyo, Bangkok, Salt Lake City, Amsterdam... I will take this opportunity to talk to him about it, this is not the kind of situation that is appropriate for email. A few days before the meeting, I informed Yoshi I wish to have a face to face discussion with him.

Mike is the manager of Takashina USA, my former boss when Stearns was in charge of the factory in Shanghai. He taught me a lot financially, we became very close. He was the sixth to learn the news, he welcomed it in a very positive way like all the others. Mike had traveled from Minneapolis to attend my 50th birthday party. 3 years already, it's so far!

Yoshi hastens to contact him to know the reason for my request, he is too afraid that I resign. Fortunately, Mike does not talk to him about anything.

We do our meeting of directors, it seems that Yoshi avoids any opportunity to meet face to face with me but I manage to jam him.

We are at the hotel bar, he orders his usual vodka-martini, exceptionally, I do the same, I'm going to need it.

The cocktail gone, I unwrap my story again and express my desire to be operated in June and September. June for hair implants, September for face feminization and vaginoplasty.

Yoshi did not expect that, he talks about his relief having feared that I resign. He asks me questions: why wait so long, unbelievable courage, he is admiring ...

Courage and admiration? I never thought of these two qualifiers about me. Like Andy, he does not mention my work, it is as a friend that he talks to me, incredible!

I approach still the subject he immediately closed by these words:

- *It's up to you to make everything work, I do not see any problem!*

Once again, tears are appearing. Yoshi was the last step at the professional level, my professional future is now secure.

Yoshi was educated in Switzerland and the US, his mother Dorothy is American, his father is Japanese. It is far from the classic Japanese mentality. Such a thing would not have been accepted, the place of women in Japan is very different than in Europe. When they are pregnant, they do not take maternity leave, they resign, having a child should not create trouble or extra expenses for the company! That is something really difficult to understand for westerners... Let say that it's their culture.

We are four board of directors, Yoshi and Simon share the direction of the Japanese entity, Mike and I are the other two. Very few companies in Japan open their doors to foreigners, they are very insular or even xenophobic. Yoshi was very clear:

- *If you are a board director it's because nobody in Japan would not dare say anything if I do something wrong.*

This has nothing to do with a traditional Japanese speech, I have a lot of chances to work for them.

Still the hardest thing to do: my parents, my sisters, my daughter. How are they going to take this? On my next trip to France, I will tell them about it face to face!

CHAPTER 12

I TELL JEANNETTE ABOUT MY DISCUSSION WITH YOSHI. For her, this is bad news, she hoped for reticence on his part. The five-year deadline has just been changed to two months. Nothing is opposed to my schedule except her, all arguments will be good to postpone this deadline, the tension is at its maximum. She needs to talk to someone, she needs someone to support her, which I understand perfectly.

Unfortunately, she chooses to talk to Gaby, her friend but also the mother-in-law of my sister Bénédicte. Gaby and Jean are the parents of Martin, my sister's husband, we know each other very well, they are part of the family.

The problem lies in the large capacity of Gaby to relay information more or less confidential. The risk that my parents will learn from her is big, very big, I have to react.

It is no longer possible to wait for my next trip, I must do this from a distance, what a horror ... Tell parents that their son will become a girl by email! It's so bad!

I must first inform my sister Bénédicte who has trouble understanding, she has never seen anything, felt nothing. I send her a long email, trying to be as accurate as possible. We talk about it, she asks me questions, expresses her surprise and difficulty in imagining her brother become her sister.

... So obviously it's a shock, the surprise is very big since nothing was visible.

- *That said, although it will certainly take time to understand that you are a girl and use your new name, our relationship will remain unchanged. It will certainly be the same for our 3 sons and Martin. But what I want to tell you is that you have to think carefully about how you will announce it to parents. I am ready to do it with you, to protect you but also them...*

Explain to your parents, in writing, the story of a life, the life of their son who wishes to become their daughter. Is there anything more difficult? I take my time to write my text, read and reread, I send it to Bénédicte for opinion, I edit, it is ready.

Bénédicte goes to my parents' home to help them get through this, luckily, she is here, we do not know how they will react. Her arrival is synchronized with the sending of my e-mail.

My dear parents,

Be seated and take the time to read this email. I would have a thousand times preferred to talk to you face to face but I fear that the information comes from another source, which I would regret it. Rest assured, I'm very healthy. All this will certainly shock you but you will understand that it is not a choice. I am very happy that Bénédicte is close to you, her support is appreciable.

I do not know if you remember but I was hospitalized at the age of 19 because of intense sternum pain, that's when I was diagnosed with ankylosing spondylitis, for this it was necessary to make a karyotype to check the different chromosomes and in particular the presence of HLA B27 antigen. That's when I was told that I had a major genetic malformation: "it's funny, you're genetically female, you're XX on chromosome 23" (men are XY, women XX). I learned quite recently that there was one case for every 50,000 births. This has the consequence of being either sterile or to have sperm of very poor quality. This probably explains the problems of Anais but I was never told anything about it at the time.

I remember that at the age of 6, I wanted to be a girl but I realized that something was wrong and that it had to be kept secret. This need was already very strong in adolescence and I took refuge in the sport to avoid thinking about it, without much success ... Once I left home, I thought I could finally live it more freely but I was deceiving myself.

When I met Jeannette (already more than 20 years ago), I spoke to her immediately, I did not want to go on bad grounds. For 20 years, she supported me and accepted me as I am, I had the opportunity to be the woman I wanted but only in the privacy of our home and it was already good.

What changed a lot of things in my life was my thyroid surgery. When I had my internal bleeding, I remember it as if it was yesterday from my last breath. I was in respiratory and cardiac arrest, it was well and truly over until I was resuscitated. I approached this death with a serenity that still troubles me today and it does not happen a day without me thinking about it. I was never able to live as I did and it was not bad to leave. Although it is not a disease, the pain is immense and continuous, spondylitis is nothing in comparison.

I stopped drinking, I changed my eating habits until I lost 25kg and at the same time, I started a treatment under the control of my doctor which consists of stopping the production of the male hormone (testosterone) and taking the female hormone (estrogen). It's been two years since I took this treatment and the changes are already visible, I have more than respectable breasts, all the hairs fell, the shape of the body changes and my character becomes more emotional.

I see a psychologist for several months, which helps me a lot. My goal was to wait a few years, stop working and make the necessary changes to finally start living. Recent events and a sentence I received like a bolt from a movie said:

"The fear of dying is nothing beside that of not living."

I am absolutely not afraid to die, I have already known that and it will happen anyway, however, I am terrified of not living. So, I decided to wait no longer and go for it. I started talking to close friends and then I continued to talk about it at work with the management staff, my colleague in the USA and my bosses. Of all, I received support that I did not even imagine, I bowled over more than once, I could not believe it. My two bosses really spoke to me as friends and it touched me a lot, there is no obstacle now. Moreover, at work, the situation becomes really difficult, everyone sees that there are big changes, physically, I am half-man, half- woman.

In the coming months, I will perform several surgical operations: hair implants, surgery of feminization of the face and finally a vaginoplasty that will finally allow me to have the body that corresponds to my mind.

I do not want to hurt anyone, I just want to start living MY life and finally be happy, I want to get rid of that body that has NEVER been mine. For you parents, of course it's not easy to hear but I think the most important thing is the happiness of your children, right? Once again, this is not a choice, it is a necessity, it's something I experienced for so many years.

All this will not be without pitfalls, without transphobia but it is not a choice, it becomes a vital necessity. Of course, it is not easy for Jeannette either who will be married to a woman. I have never been attracted to men and nothing will change for me with regard to Jeannette. The hardest is of course to feel the gaze of the family and other French people fastened about me, abroad, all this is much easier. Although it's difficult for Jeannette, she supports me and I'm clear that I want to finish my days with her.

I will be soon 53, I cannot continue to hide permanently, to lie and especially not live my life...

I shared my situation with my whole work environment, I do not do anything with my head down, everything is prepared and calculated. You must know that I never do anything randomly.

Well, everything is said, it is surely difficult for you to imagine that you will have three girls instead of two, it has always been the case but you did not know it. Bénédicte and Stéphanie are aware, I informed them this week. Bénédicte was very surprised but she supports me entirely, she has already talked to the boys who took it very well too. I just hope it will be the same for you, it would hurt me a lot if it generated a conflict between us.

If you have time, I would like you to watch this video, I identify myself 100% with this person:

https://www.youtube.com/watch?v=AWd3-aWlotE

I am available on Skype whenever you want and I hope we can talk about. Do not be sad, be happy that I can finally begin my life

Hugs

Dad, you're so beautiful

Christophe

The dice are thrown, I wait for the call of my sister, a real torture, my stomach is tied in knots, I really hope everything goes well. Finally, a message from Bénédicte,

- *Everything is fine, I go back home and we talk to each other.*

Everything is fine !!! awesome, if Bénédicte sends me this message is that really everything went well ... what a relief.

45 minutes later, I call her, the parents took it, especially my father, it's more difficult for mom who wonders if they missed something, feel guilty for not having seen anything or even suspected.

I call them, mom answers:

- *Of course, it will be difficult at first, I do not know if I can call you Céline. But why did not you say anything during all these years? Anyway, you are our son or our daughter and you will never be rejected for what you are ...*

To hear these words, you imagine the tears ... what a relief, what a liberation, that is so good. We still talk a little but we must let water flow under the bridge, it takes time to digest the information, analyze and try to understand. Of course, none of this is self-evident or easy, I'm very lucky...

So far, absolutely no one has rejected, resisted or disapproved. Nothing, absolutely nothing negative, it's just amazing.

Now comes Anais, my daughter. I inform Annie of my decision, it is not really a surprise, she knew that it could or would happen. This led to our separation and of course, it is a very bad memory, the fear of reliving it resurfaces. In addition, she is rightly worried about how Anaïs will react.

She talks to her about it, my sister Bénédicte does the same thing a few days later, no special reaction, she is surprised of course but completely in the acceptance. It will be necessary to see how she will react once the operations are carried out, for the moment, all this is rather abstract.

The last step is to inform my team of managers. It's during a regular meeting on Monday afternoon that I tell them the news.

My two friends Hieu and Hang are already aware, I had already spoken to them. The girls are smiling, their boss will be a woman, all the better, the men are mostly indifferent. The information is relayed at all levels of the staff, several reactions are completely unexpected. On my floor, several girls cried, I thought they appreciated my male side but no, not at all.

One of them said to me:

- *But how did you live so long with a so heavy secret?*

So surprising and touching, these Vietnamese are really fantastic, they will never cease to amaze me. I know for a fact that in France, things would not have happened at all in the same way.

Curiously, one of the managers comes to talk to me about the future problems of the toilets! I thought they would be embarrassed that I use the same ones as they do. Not at all, they worry about the cleanliness of the place and the perception that I will have. There is no wastewater treatment plant or very few in Vietnam, toilet paper is thrown into a garbage can, never in the bowl. Ironically, I explain that I would not have my period but that I know what it is, the discomfort quickly dissipated.

Now, everyone knows, no more barriers are opposed to my project except Jeannette who collects with difficulty all this good news.

I can now contact the clinic and the surgeon that I have chosen, the appointment is made on June 1, 2017 at 2:00pm for consultation of hair implants and the reduction of the Adam's apple. To avoid an extra trip, I added this last "option". With the voice, the Adam's apple is the second thing that usually betrays transgender people. The procedure consists in opening and cutting the excess of cartilage, for 2,500 dollars this prominence disappears completely.

Jeannette and I have to spend a few days in Phuket. We meet at Bangkok airport. I'm waiting for her just after the security checks, she's coming from Zurich, I come from Hanoi. The reunion is, say ... cordial ... but without heat ... it promises!

We settle in our villa, I rent a motorcycle and a car and we are on our way to the restaurant. Of course, I talk to her about all my conversations with my sister, my parents, Yoshi and colleagues. She still does not understand why I want to go so fast, I had said five years, I have to stick to it...

I then tell her that I made an appointment and that I added the reduction of the Adam's apple to this first step. I anticipate feminization of the face and vaginoplasty by the end of September so that Jeannette can be with me.

- *But you did not tell me, why do you want to do this extra operation? you tell me nothing...*

I took the appointment yesterday ... you were on the plane! I just don't want to get too many anesthesia's.

The discussion quickly degenerated: everything is going too fast, we had said five years, it's five, I 'm not allowed to change like that... The holidays are rotten, no need to continue in this atmosphere, I change the plane tickets to return the next day to Hanoi.

The trip goes without a word, I see in her eyes a rage, hatred, I never saw her like that. Once home, she asks me to change her ticket back to France for the next day, she does not want to stay ... Great, two days she has held two days with me...

- *I married a man and it is a man I want to keep, I do not want to live with a woman.*

Said like that, it's quite understandable and nobody could blame her but during the 20 years of our life together, she's always seen me as a woman, every day, there's nothing new but it has become concrete, real. She thought I would never dare to talk to my parents about it. Living with a woman poses a problem? Her sexual preference is clearly towards women but to admit it publicly is something else.

She leaves the next day, for the first time, I do not go to the airport, I know it's over, hard, really hard, I really did not imagine doing this road without her, she always been such a great support. This is the last time I see her in Vietnam...

Nothing prevents me now to do as I want, no more reason to wait until September to get the surgeries, she will not come. If she did, it would be to stop me.

I'm alone again in my big villa. The pain of separation and the joy of a happy future contradict each other. These moments are terrible! Fortunately, I enjoy my pool 10 months in the year, an hour of swimming and daily exercises.

The scale shows a little over 78kg, as expected, I stop smoking ... I tried to stop several times but this time it's really different. The clinic refuses to carry out any surgery if the patient is a smoker, they check during the blood test, it is frankly a sufficient motivation. The decision is much easier than expected. I lost 27kg, changing my diet, completely suppressing alcohol and with daily physical activity. I have already quit and started again twice, I know from experience that I will gain more than 10kg, that's why I wanted to lose so much, I knew they would come back ... partially!

CHAPTER 13

JUNE 3, 2017, PIYAVATE HOSPITAL. I do not recognize the place, I'm probably in the recovery room, I'm thirsty, so thirsty, nobody around me. I do not feel any pain, neither in the face nor in the abdomen. On the other hand, I feel a huge bandage that encloses my head.

Someone passes nearby:

- *Please give me something to drink, I'm so thirsty*
- *In your room!*

My bed moves finally, I make the path in the opposite direction. It's no longer a party like going, an anesthetic awakening is never fun, I'm completely groggy.

Drink, I can finally drink, my mouth is so dry, water... so good. While drinking my glass, I see the clock in my room, 6:30pm!!! It's impossible, I went to the block just after 10 am, what happened?

I'm trying to understand, it's something extremely complicated when the anesthetic fluid continues to flow through your veins. I lift the covers to try to see something. Good news, there is also a bandage, my legs are kept apart by the width of the dressing.

A soup and fruits, by experience, the first meal after an operation allows you to feel immediately better, once again it is the case, I appreciate each spoon which for a hospital soup is frankly good. However, opening the mouth is painful, it pulls from everywhere! Especially do it gently ... do not break anything, tear nothing.

I fall asleep and wake up several times, the night is long, full of questions but in view of the bandages, I must have a vagina instead of three-piece service.

Despite a well-stocked breakfast, waking is delicate, I feel that my eyes are very swollen, I really have trouble opening them. Without being really painful, all the movements seem complicated. I take a selfie to see what I look like ... I have never done a selfie in my life, I'm a woman for a few hours and it starts already? Despite the difficulties in moving my face, I cannot help but smile.

Oh, what a horror, the bandage around my head is huge, when I look at my face more closely, I see three mouths, my eyes are so swollen that they form lips, I look more like a Martian ... um, a female Martian!

I send messages to everyone to say that I am awake and everything went well. I complained about the presence of relatives just after an operation, today they are 10,000 km away and I would like to have them by my side.

I do not even want to watch TV, I prefer to rest, it is absolutely necessary to sleep, it is the best way to recover. When I'm sick or have had an operation, I get into a mode that I call "recovery". Sometimes it allows me to sleep 20 hours in the day and to have fully recovered the next day ... I have to do the same thing.

The entrance of Dr. Sutin in my room has the effect of waking me instantly, I will finally know!!!

- *Everything went well, no problem, no complications, the construction of the neo-vagina took 3:30, your face took 6:30.*

I stayed in the block from 10:30 to 17:30, the surgeon must stay focused throughout this period, it's just amazing. I understand better why I arrived so late in my room ... It's good to hear these words. Cherry on the cake, it takes away this huge bandage, I have nothing around the head, I feel breathing again I need to keep freeze packs on my face as often as possible.

I take another selfie, I still need to memorize all these moments. Without bandages, it's even worse, an alien coupled with a zombie. It hurts me to laugh, in a few days, we will not see anything, drugs to fight against swelling are generally effective just like ice.

Monday is a long day, nothing happens, no one to talk to, it's hard, being in this hospital room thousands of miles away from the family. Jeannette is not there, she repeated that she does follow me in my choices!

There is no point to over think, I had what I wanted no? I'm thinking of lots of future situations, how am I going to manage them as a woman, how to appear, how will I be perceived?

The choice I made, change of life overnight, was it the right one? Anyway, we cannot go back, it's up to me to make it work. I've always loved new challenges, but this one is the challenge of a lifetime. I have waited so long that I am not allowed to doubt or give up. It's now that everything starts, that's where I have to show that I'm strong...

D-Day +1, the next morning, I get a full sponge bath, humm as it is good, my smell mixed with different products and bandages became unbearable. In fact, it is the dressing that I have between the legs which is at the origin of these smells ... It begins to irritate me seriously.

Two nurses support me, I stand up and take a few steps ... each new step is a step towards healing.

In the afternoon, I finally see Dr. Burin ... He is rather miser in comments, the opposite of Dr. Sutin but that does not detract from his competence. He confirms that everything went very well, that there should not be any problems for the recovery. At my request, he agrees to remove this filthy dressing, a huge layer that seems to weigh several pounds ... This was only for the next day but obviously it is not a problem. Here I am with a light dressing much more pleasant.

He will return tomorrow for different care, the urinary catheter will be removed within two days...

I am now walking in the corridors; the walk is hesitant but it is necessary to move a little ... The rolling IV bag hanger and the urinary pocket acts as cane. I notice that on the doors there is no western name, I am the only one. Two rooms are obviously occupied by Kuwaitis, the flag is there... with a prohibition to return for women... ridiculous, lamentable! That's when I realize that I cannot enter there either. All the better, these people who respect women so little do not deserve we pay attention to them, even if they are overflowing with money. There are many Muslims in Thailand, especially in the islands and the south of the country. All communities live in harmony, it shows, it feels, no overflow or proselytism, the king is the cement of the country, not religion.

I probably walked two hundred meters, I'm happy with myself but it's like weights of several kilos hang between my legs. After such a personal feat, a good nap is essential.

D-day + 2, as planned, Dr. Burin makes a visit again. Delicately, he removes the last dressing, looks carefully around, he does not say anything, he cleans, looks again ... The main enemy of this surgery is necrosis, dead tissues become black, if this is the case, a new intervention is necessary.

- *Everything is fine, I will remove the gauze that is inside and I also remove the urinary catheter, it heals very well.*

He pulls on something, it's meters of gauze coming out of my belly, impressive, I feel very well this new cavity in my lower abdomen.

Removing the urinary catheter is always unpleasant but once released, one can move normally. A moment that I always look forward to especially if it is advanced a day.

It seems that he has removed everything, he still looks very carefully, as if to reassure himself.

- *You want to see?*

What do you think, of course I want to see. He moves the mirror between my legs, a flood of tears came immediately, a flood of happiness and fulfillment. It's concrete, it's there before my eyes... it does not look like anything, nothing that bodes the final appearance of a vagina but I saw so many videos about it that I knew what to expect. Dr. Burin carries out more than two hundred operations a year, he has often had to deal with this kind of emotions...

I'm on my bed, legs folded and open, five nurses arrive, they have the mission to teach me how to make an intimate cleaning with betadine. This special cleaning will be needed for a month and a half. They bring me a small plastic bag decorated with flowers, I can read "Miss Céline Audebeau", it makes emotions ... I also entitled to a special cushion in red rubber, my seat for the next weeks.

With extreme gentleness and a lot of kindness, they explain all the details by showing them several times. Their English is pretty rough, they try to explain the use of a sanitary napkin ... I had planned all that, I even had in my suitcase. I just participated in my first intimate feminine cleansing!

I am now free of any attachment, no probe, no catheter, nothing, I move freely in the corridors, I am well, I am happy but I am alone!

I sit on the toilet for my first girl pee. Beyond the emotion, it is the fear of a bad termination of the urethra: it happens that the flow of urine out in all directions, in which case it will be necessary to repeat a small intervention. It is not so, the urine falls directly into the bowl. Here I am relieved and happy...

It's June 7th, four days have passed since my operations, my first days as a woman. I slept well, more than 8 hours, after lunch, I will leave the hospital. I take my first shower, as it is delicious to feel clean. For the first time, I see my whole body in the mirror ... nothing hangs between my legs, finally ... Bruises all around the torso, impressive, I am blue and purple. My face, swollen only three days ago, begins to look like something, I can see that my features have changed while remaining the same person.

My first intimate cleaning alone is not as simple as it seems, I have no sensation in the whole area of the vagina, it will take time for all the nerve endings reconnect... intimate cleaning, it sounds so feminine!

I dress for the first time, I'm very sober, I do not feel ready to wear a dress yet. The makeup allows me to hide the remains of bruises around the eyes, the hair is loose, a beautiful cleavage, here I am ready to face my new life.

The driver will not come until early afternoon, I spotted a bakery in the hospital, a good cappuccino with a croissant, the dream. I leave my room, nurses are admiring and congratulate me, they leave all to see me... It's terrible these tears come all the time.

The smell of coffee is irresistible, I'm walking on the ground floor of the crowded hospital, visitors, patients, drivers... Everything I wanted was realized: to be transparent, nobody pays attention to me, I am a woman like the others, my god that it is good.

Coffee and croissant are just as much, now is the time for a new life.

The driver picks me up as planned, this first drive is a nightmare, every chaos of the road is fully felt and despite the special cushion.

My hotel is a few hundred meters from the PAI clinic where I will do the future medical visits, I check in with my male passport, no questions, no problems as long as the credit card works. The room is better than I imagined: an equipped kitchenette, a living room with flat screen TV, a large bedroom and a large bathroom... perfect. I will stay there for the next 15 days for my convalescence.

I need something to eat, I do not think I can go down to have breakfast in the restaurant, at least not right now.

The supermarket is much further than I imagined, it is the return that is hard, the bags in each hand seem to weigh tons. The pain between the legs becomes stronger, provided that I do not tear anything. I should never have done so much:

- *What a bitch? So stupid!*

These words came out alone, I start laughing, it hurts even more, it's my first bad words as a woman... I'm learning fast!

Installed in my room, I activate the "recovery" mode, I sleep more than 16 hours a day for three days, it avoids thinking and allows the days to pass more quickly. They are punctuated by meals, TV, emails and rest.

Jeannette takes my news by Skype, the discussion degenerates quickly, I see that $150,000 have disappeared from our account, a large part of what I had saved to take early retirement, to finally share time with her. She took everything, opened an account under her name and transferred the money. It's disgusting, I do not attach far as much importance to the money as Jeannette but still, do that on my back the day of my operation.

She is convinced that I was going to lose my job or worse, that I could have passed away. In the latter case, all the accounts would be blocked, she takes her precautions according to her terms... I was just a source of money, nothing else, that's all that interested her. Dozens of situations come to mind and I finally understand: Christophe how he could be that naive? Céline will be on her guard, relationships are broken, no need to go further, only divorce can get us out of this situation.

In the 9th day I returned to the clinic for a medical check with Dr. Burin. Boun greets me with great pleasure, he is so used to seeing happiness or suffering. The kisses I found so ridiculous on my arrival suit me perfectly today. It must have been a girl to appreciate them.

Patients with a red buoy are easily identifiable, they are also waiting for their appointment. The examination rooms are tiny, two meters by three, moreover. In the middle throne a gynecological examination chair, I undress and settle in a position quite unusual for me.

This totally immodest way of exposing me annoys me a little, how many millions of women have already felt the same thing?

He examines the interior with plenty of barbaric tools, no worries, everything is normal.

We will do the first dilation, it will be done twice a day for 20 minutes and this, all your life unless a natural dilatation.

I was perfectly informed of these dilations, but living it is very different from reading it. Feeling this object penetrate you and touch your flesh which is still bruised, it hurts ... What a strange feeling, I am penetrated for the first time in my life.

But what did he mean by natural dilatation? I did not read anything about it, how would the vagina expand naturally? It took me a while to understand but I cannot imagine a man replacing the dilatation. I wanted this sex to live in accordance my gender, it will probably never serve, this is not the goal.

The dilatations of the following days are really painful, the absorbable sutures come off everywhere, I hope they will quickly disappear.

I walk now without difficulties, I go shopping, I go to the restaurant, Celine does all this, incredible!

This is my last appointment at the clinic, this afternoon I will be going back to Hanoi, it's so hard to be alone.

The medical visit goes smoothly, I am good for the service, ready to travel. They give me documents certifying the various operations carried out in case there are problems with immigration. I fear the crossing of the Vietnamese border, hope that they will let me in.

At Bangkok airport that I know so well, I register in the area reserved for the business class, never queue and a very good welcome. My ticket in hand, I head for immigration, I extend my passport to the policeman, he looks, looks at me:

- *What is that?*

Of course, the photo did not fit anymore, I try to explain to him but his English is more than limited. I give him the documents from the clinic, unfortunately, it's also in English ... He leaves with all the documents, I did not imagine having any problem at this border. He returned 15 minutes later with a higher ranking, he had one more pin on his epaulettes. They checked the photo taken at the entrance of the country, it corresponds more to my current face. The officer takes my passport and stamps it.

- *Excuse us Madam...*

Just for this "madam", it was worth to wait. I embark, the flight seems long, fortunately I can lie down. To avoid problems similar to the immigration of Hanoi, I remove jewels, earrings and makeup ... I arrive at the ticket office, I really do my dirtiest head, it hardly looks at me ... What horror, I had to hide myself as a man to pass, I hope it will be the last time.

While waiting for my suitcase, I run (a way to talk) to the toilet, I cannot go out like that. As I crossed the toilet door on the woman's side, new torrent of tears, that's it, I'm there ... Who would dream to go into the toilet and get moved? Well yes, this dream I had for so many years and now I'm here, in the most natural way...

I come out transformed, capped, lightly made up, happy simply. I pick up my suitcase, pass the customs, they never check the Westerners and I never had to hide anything. Here I am on the forecourt of the airport, I returned.

Hang, my Vietnamese friend runs to me with a bouquet of flowers, what a surprise, it makes me so happy to see her, I did not expect it, we are girlfriends now, we hold each other tightly. My very first flowers, I who love them so much and for so long. Duong, my driver, also gives me a big bouquet of roses, I'm just so happy. Hang compliments me, asks me hundreds of questions, I'm so happy to see her, the first comforting face since I left.

I do not wish anyone to live this journey alone. After the removal of the testicles, the hormonal changes are so important that they make the person extremely fragile and vulnerable, it is a real tsunami that crosses the body.

I arrive home, my two cats are excited to see me again. As a man that I left, it is as a woman that I come back!

CHAPTER 14

AS IT IS GOOD TO WAKE UP AT HOME, resume my habits, drink a good coffee, feed the two beasts... Since the beginning of my diet, my breakfast consists of a soup, the famous Vietnamese Pho.

My maid prepares it for me but for some time, I find mine much better. A big pan will do the week. I prefer it to beef, the name comes from the French stew, like what the French did not do only bad things in the time of the colonies. It is also the only Asian country that consumes so much bread because of the French presence.

When I go to the local market, it is not uncommon to meet elderly people with the Basque beret and happy to be able to exchange a few words in French. I was born ten years after the defeat at Dien Bien Phu, the withdrawal of the French. Since the six years that I live here, I have never felt any animosity or resentment towards the French.

They like to say that the French have built everything and the Americans destroyed everything. They also say that they never lost a war. As long as this lasts, recent tensions with China are not reassuring. China claims that all the waters of the China Sea belong to them, from southern China to northern Malaysia. Japan, Taiwan, the Philippines, Vietnam, Indonesia and Malaysia are in territorial conflict with the Chinese. Not a single Western government dares to lift a finger when the communist giant takes over new territories ...

My first task at home is to clean my clothes. It takes a whole room, women's clothes accumulated for years but have never seen the light of day. First of all, remove all the masculine clothes, I cannot imagine that I will not have to hide anymore, it still sounds unreal. I fill several bags, what a joy to get rid of all that!

I also remove women's "non-wearable" clothes: long dresses, formal wear or sexy lingerie that I will never have the opportunity to wear. Thach, my housekeeper, gets all these clothes, I think she has to sell some of it, she does what she wants.

It's been two years since she comes to clean every afternoon. Her French is really good, if only I spoke Vietnamese as well ... I tried to learn it but it is so complicated ... The Chinese side is very simple, that is to say in comparison...

She was not really comfortable when I told her about my change, I saw her embarrassed. I'll see her this afternoon ... she will have to adapt to it.

The dressing room looks great, a lot of space is released. No worries, I know that the gaps will soon be filled.

The second important thing of the day is to take an appointment at the embassy. Since the justice modernization law (law n ° 2016-1547 of November 18, 2016), it is a civil servant who authorizes the change of first name, it is not more necessary to go through the court, my appointment is for the next day.

The administrative marathon will take months, I am prepared:

- First of all, the change of first name
- Request for change of sex from the High Court
- Modification of the birth certificate
- New passport and identity card
- New resident visa
- Change of the social security number
- Social security card change
- Pension fund change
- Bank changes
- Driver's license
- ...

My list includes more than 40 lines and I certainly forget some.

A new difficult step, going out shopping, facing the eyes of those who will recognize me. Dr. Sutin had been very clear: he feminizes the face by softening his features, he does not "make" in any case a new face. He advises me to go see another surgeon if that was my wish.

My image in the mirror always sends me back to the same person, even if the features are softened. I cannot imagine the difficulty of receiving a new face, how to accept oneself? This image satisfies me fully, I see a woman, there is no doubt. Surgery contributed a lot to this metamorphosis but I remain convinced that there was an internal explosion of femininity, that lots of doors suddenly opened.

Facing the eyes of others has always been my biggest fear, I have no choice, I cannot continue to live hidden.

When I enter the small grocery store in the street opposite, the owner looks at me from head to toe. Obviously, she has trouble understanding ... he disguises himself?

Arrival at the cash desk:

- *You need something else mister?*

This "mister" slaps like a slap, it is not today that you will consider as a woman.

The butcher shop is too far away, I take my bike ... what a mistake. Sitting directly on wounds with roadways always broken, torture. Crossing the door, the two saleswomen are taken aback, the manager comes to me and wraps her arms around my waist:

- *You're so beautiful!*

Incredible reaction, they jump like kids by tapping in their hands, they look so happy ... What a contrast with the previous store ... usual scenario, tears are again appearing.

The third store where I am less familiar:

- *Good Morning Madam*

As it is sounds so nicely this "madam", that this music is sweet ... that's it, I'm there.

When Thach discovers me in the afternoon, she also gratifies me with a "hello ma'am" but this one did not come from the heart. I quickly tell her about my operations and how I'm going to live now.

- *And madam - speaking of Jeannette - she does not come anymore?*
- *No, she will not come anymore.*

A big "YES" came from the heart escapes her, it is punctuated by a gesture of victory of the arm. I really did not expect it, it seemed to me that they got along well...

- *Madam, she is always behind me to check what I'm doing.*

The rest of the day goes to bed, you have to spare the machine, recover...

The next day, my driver is waiting for me as planned, my appointment at the embassy is at 9:30. Duong drives me to the factory every day for six years, I thought that after driving daily in China, I could ride everywhere ... I was wrong. Driving in Vietnam is completely crazy, it is a conduct of avoidance permanently, the accident is close at all times. It is the politics of everyone for themselves, what is behind me does not concern me. Even children never look at what comes from behind before crossing or cycling, a real suicide, a constant lottery.

Duong gratifies me with a "waouh", he is a real macho who rolls mechanics, who always speaks louder than the others and who has delicate gestures like an elephant. However, he has a heart of gold, I am often invited in his family, he is a very good driver and always available. He finds me beautiful ... amazing, I did not imagine that of him ... all the better for that.

I wear a black silk tank top and white cropped trousers, nothing ostentatious for my first meeting with the administration. When I made an appointment, I explained the context of the visit. It's my turn:

- *Madam Audebeau?*
- *Yes, it's me!*

I really note the attention of the official, what tact, to the civil status I am still "Mister".

She makes no comment, she explains that the competent civil registrar is in Nantes (Brittany), in general, all that concerns expatriates is in this city.

We fill out the form, I enclose a copy of the letter of the clinic detailing the surgeries performed. I prepared a handwritten letter explaining the reasons for my approach as well as my first photos of identity as a woman.

For the first time, I write Céline on an official document... My second male given name is that of my godfather, Alain, my father's brother. I hesitate to put a second, that of my godmother, she would be happy! And then no, so many documents to fill each time a border is crossed, let's make short...

Imagine that two days later, I receive an official document informing me of the decision of my first name change. I'm now called Celine!

- *... therefore, you are now allowed to be called Celine.*

I read this sentence more than ten times, as it is sweet to read this name, I chose it at the age of 12, at 53 it becomes mine. Well, there is still written Mr. Celine but it will be the next step.

This document is sent to the city hall where I was born for the update of my birth certificate. When the certificate will be in my hands, I'll be able to request a new passport with an updated photo and my new first name...

And say that we talk about administrative delays, being at the end of the world and receive a decision two days later! Unbelievable!

I give myself a week to rest, I plan to return to work three weeks after my operation, it is unexpected, in general, we talk about 6 to 8 weeks. I have the advantage of deciding on my schedule, if it did not work, I could stay at home. In addition, I can sit and avoid any unnecessary effort.

Many things in everyday life are new, we do not walk in the same way, the vocabulary changes, we sit differently, we hold a glass otherwise ... Tons of small details that we cannot imagine.

There is no manual or operating instruction that explains how to become a woman overnight. I chose to do it this way, it's up to me to adapt quickly.

Even to pee, you have no explanation, I happened to stand in front of the toilet and rummage in my pants ... nothing ... I turn around and sit down I guess this old reflex goes quickly disappear, at least I hope so.

I go shopping in a small shopping center, the "Gourmet" store offers all the French products that we need. The range of cheese is impressive, just as much as prices. 30€ for a small portion of raclette cheese, you really have to appreciate it.

A huge storm echoed for more than thirty minutes, terrible tropical rains. No way to get home, my bike is in the basement and there is 20 cm of water on the road. I just need to be patient by sitting on a terrace and drinking good tea. I now wait in front of the door and look at the rain that does not weaken. A man comes towards me and begins to speak to me in an approximate English.

But who is this guy? What's his problem?

My killer eyes took him away. I realize that he comes to talk to the woman, flirt with me, I have to calm down, it's rather flattering.

The dilations become less painful over time, I get to 6 inches deep (just over 15cm). The average length of the dear French male penis is 13.5 cm. However, if you interrogate the guys separately, they all have more than 20 cm, as virility requires!

Anyway, I do not think this new sex will ever be used, but I do not want it to close.

CHAPTER 15

JUNE 26, 2017, THIS DAY IS THE ONE for which I am most apprehensive: the return to the factory. I'm going to confront 420 people who are wondering what I'm going to look like.

In the aftermath of my operations, alone in my hotel room, I tried to prepare myself for this day: how will I be welcomed, what will become of my authority? Jokes? Rejects? So many questions without answers.

The first difficulty of the day: how to dress? My two friends Hang and Hieu want to see me as feminine as possible, wear a dress or skirt. I'm not ready, a kind of blockage. Although with my six feet tall and my 84 kilos, I am far from female top model and even further from Vietnamese who consider themselves fat when they exceed 50k... I need time to get used to this new image and break everything that was forbidden to me before.

I opt for sobriety again, pink cropped trousers, a cotton and lace top and discreet sandals. Light makeup, a ponytail, here I am ready. Gordon, our American customer, the first person I talked to about my transition, is in Hanoi for a few days. It's been just four months since I told him about my planned transition planned for five years later, in a sense I understand Jeannette when she says that everything is going too fast. Four months ago, I was talking about it for the first time, today I am a woman.

I stand in the street waiting for my driver, what happiness to live in broad daylight. Gordon is in the car, he congratulates me on the change, he did not imagine that my change would be so fast. We talk about everything and nothing during the 45-minute trip ... The stress rises, must I go in each office or I stay in mine to wait for people to come?

We are ten minutes from the factory, Duong, my driver, has already had 3 calls, curious! At the approach of the factory, it is he who calls ... If only I understood a little what he says ... I'm afraid they prepare me something! I question Gordon, he says he does not know anything. My heart beats hard, very hard, I'm terrified, my first big test.

At the entrance of the factory building, the home screen displays "Welcome Miss Céline": nice but I'm worried. I go up the few steps, it smells like a trap, the offices are empty, not the least noise. Gordon goes off on his side, I go to my office at the end of the hall. The purchasing and sales offices are empty too, so, where are they?

I open the door of my office, cries, applause, confetti, they are thirty. Ouch, ouch, ouch, what a slap! I stay planted like an idiot, with my hand on my mouth and my eyes wet. Frankly, I did not expect it, Julien offers me a bouquet of flowers and makes me a kiss, the first of a man. I get a necklace from Hang's hands, I'll learn that everyone has participated... What emotion, more flowers, tears of joy. I see Gordon at the entrance of the office, he knew, he did not spill the beans. My meeting table is filled with fruit and a cake on which I read "welcome Céline, be yourself, be happy!". Everyone speaks to me, asks questions, finds me beautiful ... they are not really objective but it is the attention that counts. We stay over an hour to eat, discuss, laugh ... Thinking that I feared this moment, this moment that I feared most will probably be one of the best memories of my new life.

It remains to go around the factory, managers are already converted to my cause, what about all workers?

I open the door that leads to the staircase that dominates the main workshop, everyone gets up and applauds me ... This is not true, I do not remember having felt such an emotion before. Some sewers come to hold me in their arms, some men have prepared flowers, how to resist that? The Vietnamese are not fake, they have the culture of the smile, it is a chance to live among them.

My god, what a day, it goes without saying that I'm far away from the idea I had of that day. For sure, it will remain etched forever, the video of the reception is even on YouTube... so nice to relive this moment. I realize by watching that my voice is not great, there is still a lot of work to do with Tiphaine.

In the days that follow, the director of the factory bank comes to me with a huge arrangement of flowers... He is new, he looks at me with a lot of attention. I discuss grievances that I have never managed to get with his predecessors. He accepts all of it, all that has been refused me after long and tedious negotiations is accepted today, incredible! The power of women!

Our main subcontractor brings me beautiful flowers and high-quality beauty products. Thereafter, the factory landlord will do the same.

So many flowers, I love it, of course I have ever received so many. What a pleasure to feel accepted, respected and considered.

I go back to the Embassy to get my new passport, my first name Céline is printed there, right next to my family name and my new photo ... what a change. I have been traveling for a long time with two passports. Sometimes the Chinese visa application takes from a week to ten days. During this period, it is impossible for me to travel which is very disabling.

As I look at this new passport with so much pleasure, I realize that I will not be able to use it for traveling. My Vietnam resident permit is in the name of Christophe. I cannot leave the country with an air ticket on behalf of Celine and a visa on behalf of Christophe.

I have to change my second passport by keeping Christophe but changing the photo... In less than a week I get the new sesame. I now have two passports, one with Christophe and the other with Céline, both with my new face but still as a male.

The consulate proposed me to act as intermediary for my request for gender change. Testimonials, certificates and photos are necessary to complete this file. Hervé, my doctor, wrote a sex change certificate. The consulate gives me a document certifying that I am presenting myself as a woman at the embassy.

The request is addressed to the President of the high court on which I depend. No need for a lawyer, it's just necessary to provide all certificates, testimonials and photos that prove your new state. Since the new French simplification law, the sex reassignment surgery is no more required, even sterilization is not necessary. I understand very well all those people who do not want to go through surgery, my choice was different. I send the complete file to the high court of Nantes by the diplomatic bag hoping for a quick settlement.

I could have my resident visa changed by using Céline but that involves changing all the legal documents of the company. I will wait for the gender change to do it, no need to undertake twice a procedure that will certainly be complex...

I need this passport and this visa for a close deadline, it makes me frankly afraid ... to pass immigration of the United States. I think there is no other country where immigration is so painful to cross. By definition, if you are a foreigner, you are either a terrorist or you come to take the work of the Americans.

I take my ticket, Hanoi / Seoul / Los Angeles and finally Salt Lake City in Utah, the capital of the Mormons. For French citizens, visa is not required, it is however necessary to complete the ESTA for permission to enter the territory.

We are at the end of July 2017, just two months since the surgeries were performed. My suitcase is ready, the ball in the stomach is only getting bigger as the deadline approaches. I travel with a feminine appearance but show this famous M on the passport that betrays your identity. As long as it changes quickly.

No worries to pass the immigration of Vietnam, what do they think when seeing my passport? The pictures correspond, after all, they think what they want, I do not care.

I travel in business class, I have a bed all the way, no pain, everything is fine. Los Angeles, LAX airport, the last time I came there, I waited two hours for immigration, hope it will not last for so long, I do not see myself standing for so long.

Almost no queue, so lucky. The officer is a woman, a cold and suspicious look like all colleagues elsewhere, this should definitely be part of their training!

- *Why do you come the US?*
- *I'm attending a trade show in Salt Lake City.*
- *What do you do as a job?*
- *I am the General Manager of a factory in Vietnam that manufactures products for the USA.*
- *I see, shit from Asia!*
- *Yes, that's it - especially never contradict - The shit you buy...*

The discussion ends there, no mention of my gender, so much the better, the oval stamp so characteristic is finally affixed on my passport, phew...

I change to another terminal for my domestic flight, a big urge to pee. I follow the signs and here I am waiting in line, at least twenty women in front of me ... On the man side, nothing, the flow is completely normal. I cannot help smiling, I who wanted so much to cross this door, here I am waiting in line, too funny.

At Salt Lake City Airport, I find my American colleagues including Mike, my former boss. No special reaction, he reacts as if I have always been like that ... perfect, I did not ask for more.

Rather than going to the hotel, Yoshi has booked a large villa in Park City, a beautiful ski resort that hosted the 2002 Olympic Games. Yoshi will not come, however, his brother Simon with his whole family and his parents will be there. The house has 14 rooms, I have never seen anything similar before, the American excess, everything is giant...

Simon and his wife Naomi congratulate me on the change, the two boys are rather surprised, they do not make the link with who I was before, it is not worse.

Yoshi and Simon's parents join us for an evening meal at an excellent Italian restaurant in Park City. For the first time, I am surrounded by my colleagues in a public place. I am in a phase where I observe absolutely everything, I note all the details. I do not see any embarrassment of being in my presence, awesome. The level of tolerance of people is much higher than I imagined. Hisaya, Yoshi's father who recently retired, asks me if I'm new to the company, Dorothy his wife, kicks him:

- *But I had explained to you, you already forgot?*

General laughing!

The first day at the Outdoor Retailer show with Mike, is punctuated by various meetings with customers and suppliers. I'm in a tailor skirt, white silk blouse, high heels ... very classy, I feel good, I feel so much woman. To get my badge, I use my passport with Celine, I do not want to walk the halls with my male name.

It's amazing, most suppliers do not recognize me. For the first time, I discover misogyny, the superiority of the male. One of the vendors only speaks to Mike, but I'm the client, not Mike. I'm probably considered as his assistant, the one who does not have the right to speak during meetings. I smiled with contempt. At the end of the meeting, I let him know who I am and that he can go elsewhere, I hope it will make him think, he just lost tens of thousands of dollars in a few seconds.

I meet former American colleagues who do not recognize me either. One of them looks at me but basically talks to Mike, whom he knows well, just before leaving, I tell him:

- *You do not recognize me, do you? You came to my home in Shanghai several times, you ate there, you even made me a job offer.*

Amazement, questions, who is this chick? When I mention my former position in the Shanghai factory, the link is made ... Mouth wide open, not knowing what to say, he realizes, too funny.

Since my return to Hanoi, I discovered a formidable weapon in case of a suspicious look, the absolute weapon, the smile... When a person looks at you and apparently has doubts about your gender, you smile looking at them right in the eyes, the person in front of you is obliged to answer you with a smile that takes the place of approval, it works every time... If you ever lower your head to avoid the look, it's lost!

At the grocery store where the owner kept calling me Mr. even dressed in a skirt, I kindly said with a smile that she will not see me again if she continues to call me Monsieur. Not only does she call me Madame but she does it with a beautiful, sincere smile, she understands that my "status" will be permanent.

My colleagues have also asked me if I had done something to my teeth. No, nothing, funny question. In thinking about it, they never saw me smile until now, it's permanent!

The new prospects and customers we meet at the show do not suspect anything, I'm just a woman, everything I've always wanted. It is an enormous enjoyment to "pass", to be seen as a woman and not as a man who has made a transition.

The days are long, I discover the pleasure of removing shoes in the evening with bruised feet that request massages.

On the last day, Mike takes me shopping, the mall at Park City is huge. I go into all the shops, bags accumulate, Mike stays outside and acts as a porter, what happiness.

Until now, I was amazed by the tolerance of people who accept me as I am. Today, I realize that it is not, they may be tolerant but I am also perceived as a woman, there is no doubt in their eyes, it shows. It is today that I really trust myself, this fear of being unmasked has almost disappeared.

Mike at the dinner added:

- *It's hard to say so but while shopping this afternoon, Celine was the most beautiful woman in the mall.*

Wow, coming from him, it's really the ultimate compliment, besides, I know he's sincere ... And I who did not want to come to the USA...

CHAPTER 16

JUST TEN DAYS HAVE PASSED since I returned from the USA and I am already preparing for my departure for France ... Everyone and especially the family will discover Céline for the first time, are there more stressful situations? Certainly, but this is mine, a mixture of joy and fear.

Returns to France are not good memories: Usually, Jeannette was preparing me a list of work to be done. Could she not understand that I also need to rest, that my physical abilities were limited? She repeatedly said that my job as plant manager was not tiring and she could do it too! Really? Have responsibility for more than 400 people and manage millions of dollars! It's a constant pressure that is tiring but I doubt that she understands it to this day.

For the first time in a long time, I'm looking forward to returning in France. So far, the communication with my parents and Bénédicte was limited to the minimum, in summer and at Christmas. I really had nothing interesting to share. By dint of staying home to feel myself, I had shut myself up, a real antisocial. But it was not a choice, just a survival mode.

With my mother, since the announcement of my transition, we communicate every day, what a contrast! It's not the others who have changed, it's me, what's more beautiful than to love life and specially to love oneself?

I always take the same flight with Thai Airways, Hanoi - Bangkok then Bangkok - Frankfurt. The flight to Frankfurt is onboard an Airbus A380, probably the best plane on the market with the A350, so quiet that sometimes one wonders if we are moving. Because of my Platinum status, I am often upgraded in First Class. A bed of 2 meters by 70 cm with a good futon, Dom Perignon, Caviar, foie gras, wines to cry ... The service of this company is just exceptional, it's been five years since I travel with them. The staff is of a high class and always available.

We provide you pajamas, you have a large bathroom, a living room. Sometimes we regret to arrive so quickly. You can imagine the horrible conditions in which I travel.

Arriving in Frankfurt, I go to my car rental agency, it's my favorite vice, I like sport cars and the more horses, the better. One thing is certain, you cannot tax me for wanting to show my manhood. German motorways have no limitation, at least in certain sectors. I like speed, this kick in the buttocks to acceleration. BMW M series, Mercedes AMG including S63 AMG 612 horsepower, I made a peak speed of 322km / h on the speedometer ... stupid when I think about it today. It was the time when I was still a stupid dude.

Today I'm happy with a ... Ford ... A Ford Mustang GT, the beast, a 5-liter V8 engine that roars at the slightest acceleration. It's not an M4 at the acceleration level but still, there are 435 horses that grow.

I arrive quietly in Colmar around 10 am at my sister Benedict's home, no excessive speed, incredible as I became reasonable. This is the first time I'm so happy to see her. Despite all her past health problems, she was and still is an exceptional support. It is obvious that things would not have gone so well with my parents if she had not acted as an intermediary, as a buffer when she too needed to digest this change.

We discuss a thousand things, different reactions, I tell my American adventures. I have always been the big brother, I cannot imagine myself as her sister, it will come, no doubt. Martin my brother-in-law makes me a kiss, we shook hands for more than twenty years ... He did not think, it came naturally, great!

My parents are invited for dinner, the first time they will discover their daughter. How to dress? Bénédicte provides very good advice, black skirt and sleeveless top very feminine, better to show myself without excess.

My parents arrive, they are warned, they are ready, no particular reaction. I'm so happy to see them, we have a great evening, everyone is happy, me first. To be so with my people was beyond all my hopes.

The next day is devoted to shopping, Benedicte takes her elder sister, just incredible to walk in the city of my adolescence, my studies, I walk as a happy woman and go shopping with my sister. This also I had not imagined!

We go to Sephora, a makeup shop, I have plenty of things to buy even if I do not know what I need yet:

- *Hello Ladies!*

Benedicte jumps, yes, she speaks of us both, these words are so sweet. On several occasions the same scene is repeated, we laugh about it. For people who know me, Christophe became

Céline. We can do whatever we want, we always see the person I was before, difficult to ignore it. For people who do not know me, I am a woman and this without any doubt. That's hard to understand, even for myself.

What a day, full of shops, already enough to fill a new suitcase, madness but the event was important, I could not deprive myself of these many purchases ... And then damn, why should I justify myself I am free and happy, I have to enjoy it.

I occupy the room of my nephew and godson Lucas, a future great filmmaker to no doubt. Well, he has no more a godfather but two godmothers, it's not commonplace.

Tomorrow I go to sleep at my parent's home, after more than 25 years, I go back to sleep in my parent's home. Tonight, I'm invited with Fabienne and Michel. They live in the village next to my home, my former home. Michel is a figure, a hunter, a fisherman, big mustache, a large belly, a language more chastened, an inveterate flirt, sometimes macho but a guy with the heart of gold. You have to know him, a golden guy.

For his 50 years birthday, I offered him 15 days of fishing in Thailand. We're speaking about fresh-water monster fishes, the grail for any fisherman, an event he would never have afforded and I enjoy sharing, that's what the money is for, to convert it into happiness no? His son Anthony will join the trip, many huge fishes of all species, paradise and then THE fish, the fish of a lifetime. After an hour of fighting, Michel catches a carp of almost 80kg, probably in the top 5 worldwide. Something that will only happen once in a lifetime. The guy who has the world record with 86kg, it's me ... it did not last, but still. We had a wonderful holiday. The variety of fish was just amazing, carps, red tails, Mekong catfishes, Arapaima's, giant piranhas. Fabienne is more reserved, it is difficult or impossible for her to leave home more than two days. Anthony is in senior year, the teenager who discovers his first love.

Arriving, the first thing to look at is my car, Anthony is crazy about the Ford Mustang. Naturally, he makes me a kiss, so surprising, the last time he gave me the kisses, he must have been 10 years old.

Fabienne is struggling, she does not understand why I did that, she cries. I try to explain to her as simply and quickly as possible. She sees my smile, she sees how happy I am. The macho mustache guy did not change his behavior, he told me:

- *We are friends for a long time, it's not because you will become a chick that it will change.*

We're having a great evening, Fabienne's tensions have dissipated, I think she understood. She worries about Jeannette.

Jeannette, I saw her for the first time this afternoon, what she had always seen of me is now in the open, I have nothing to hide.

Words have trouble coming, she wants to remake the past, "you told me this, you told me that..." We cannot go back, it's done, what's the point of remaking the story with so many "if". The discussion degenerates quickly, I am the cause of all her evils, it is necessary to divorce. I'm not against it but it's not the moment to talk about it: too many emotions, too much pain on both sides, I have to leave, I'm no longer at home. Have I ever been?

The next day, another test awaits me and not least: look for Anais, my daughter.

I'm dressed lightly, silk shorts and white lace T-shirt. Opening the door of the apartment:

- *Wow dad, you're so beautiful!*

Can we hope for softer and more sincere words? I do not think so, they will remain engraved forever. I hug her in my arms. We communicated via Skype when I was still in Hanoi.

- *I changed outside but I'm your daddy and will always stay, absolutely nothing changed, I just needed to become a girl to feel good.*
- *No problem!*

Indeed, no problem, not the least, Annie is there, reassured, smiling, happy to see Anaïs bloomed. Her anxieties were really legitimate but I could not imagine Anaïs taking it badly. She sees very well that the person in front of her is the same.

We go to my parents where we will stay a few days.

Long discussions, many things to explain going back to my five years. That they have not seen anything for all these years, is not easy to understand and accept. Yet they did not do anything wrong, on the contrary, it's just the fault of no luck. At no time have I made the slightest choice, I have suffered since my earliest childhood. Society imposes to stay in the closet, this kind of thing does not show itself.

In any case, it's a real pleasure to be with them. My father's is the first to call me Céline ... it's amazing, these tears come all the time, really a girl thing. Mom does the same in the most natural way. They have trained, it is not possible!

I leave with Anaïs to spend three days in Amnéville, a spa town, it's nice to enjoy moments just both of us, walk, play ... She loves going to the restaurant, she falls in love with the Buffalo

Grill, the great kitchen! She's thin as a wire, eating fries with ketchup will not really affect her... not the same for me!

We visit the zoo which is huge, shopping, cinema, restaurant, aquarium, all good times. We had three beautiful days. Once back, we go to a Japanese restaurant with Annie, her mother. We are sitting all three, Anaïs is really happy with both parents. She calls me daddy most naturally, Annie suggests that she calls me Celine when we are at the restaurant. A very nice evening, Annie evokes the bad memories brought to the surface, here she is reassured but she still cannot call me Celine, too difficult!

For Anaïs, it's quite the opposite, she becomes and enforcer if someone calls me Christophe by mistake, she corrects them immediately, my most fervent supporter.

I had 15 days of real vacation, a lot of emotions, a lot of good things, a real treat.

I return to Hanoi, another deadline is very near, in three days I go to Bangkok for the reconstruction of the nose and the reduction of the Adam's apple. I am not at all a fan of cosmetic surgery but it is really necessary for me to feel comfortable, fully feminine.

Dad, you're so beautiful

CHAPTER 17

AUGUST 24, 2017, I am again sitting in the lounge of Hanoi Airport, same chair as at the previous BIG departure but not at all with the same anxiety. The icing on the cake, I'm now on the woman side to the toilets, I cannot help but smile broadly every time I walk through this door.

Once in Bangkok, I find the same driver as the last time, he does not find the same person, he has trouble recognizing me. We go straight to the hotel, the same as last time, I only have an appointment at the clinic in the afternoon. This time, all the preliminary exams are no longer necessary.

My room, although not on the same floor, is exactly the same. I quickly do some shopping, eat a sandwich and get ready for the clinic...

Boun calls me to inform me of the postponement of the appointment, I have all the afternoon for me. I jump in a cab to Central World, one of the biggest shopping centers I've ever visited. I am sure I will find something on which to spend my Thai bahts. I go from shop to shop, I go from one fitting room to another, I find some clothes in my size, something a little complicated in Asia in general.

It's so nice to be able to touch, try, buy ... Everything that was forbidden before, I looked from a distance, I bought without trying, too worried that they might suspect something ... What a change!

I go through a makeup shop Sephora, I find of course what was missing, I go to checkout. A beautiful trans girl takes care of me, I recognize them easily enough now. The Thai's have bodies that allow them to appear feminine naturally, no surgery of the face is required. On the other hand, I see the prominent Adam's apple, which confirms my suspicions

- *Do you need something else?*

What a horror, such a beautiful girl with a strong male voice. Mine is not yet at the top but still not at this point. Too bad she does not make efforts. My voice is still perfectible, what I just heard is most motivating.

I spend a quiet evening in my room, I cook fried vegetables with chicken, a Vietnamese recipe that I adore.

I sit in front of the TV and proceed to my daily dilation. The scars are almost invisible, the hair has grown back, the appearance is remarkable, in every way identical to a so-called biological woman, I say "so called" because biologically, I am also a woman. The vulva is in all respects comparable to the female sex.

Tonight, the feeling is different, the pain has completely disappeared, I even begin to feel pleasure. I insist a little ... ohhhhhh, incredible, my first orgasm, how is it possible?

I'm totally upset, I do not understand what's happening to me. I have read tons of things about it, but I have never been to the pleasure section. I wanted this sex to live in accordance with my gender, I was miles away from thinking that I would enjoy it. I jump on my computer and actually read that when the operation is well done, orgasms are possible in 50% of cases

It's so different from what I knew before, no comparison and furthermore, it's ten times stronger. September 3rd, it's been three months to the day that I had surgery and today I had pleasure. I have a hard time recovering, a door that I didn't expect suddenly opens. I drew a line about sex, no problem no longer having pleasure but there ... An incredible emotion, an unexpected surprise.

After a night on a floating cloud, I still have that blissful smile of the day before, so unlikely.

I wear a blue silk top, very light, cleavage, I love it. Bottom, an off-white straight skirt just above the knees and beige heels ... classy, I feel good in this outfit.

The driver is waiting for me, the clinic is only 600 meters, the journey is very fast. Through the transparent window, I see Boun moving, always the same ... I open the door, I smile, he drops his cup filled with water.

- *Oh my God, oh my god ...*

But what does he have, what takes him? The whole reception is coming to his side. They put their hands on their mouths in a very stylish way ... let say exaggerated ...

- *You're so beautiful, a real lady!*

Wow, they have seen many trans in their clinic, I appreciate the compliment, I know it comes from the heart ... I do not escape their kisses that I found so silly. Today, they rejoice me. They look at me, touch me make me turn ... what a success!

Upstairs, some nurses recognize me and stay surprised. I did not expect it, but I must admit, I am very proud of the effect I produce. Dr. Sutin gratifies me with a:

- *Oh, so nice!*

My smile is omnipresent, how to do otherwise with so many compliments. I do not dream, we compliment the woman I have become!

The doctor explains to me by his very well executed drawings how he will proceed for both surgeries. The reduction of the Adam's apple takes only a few minutes. Some clinics do this under local anesthesia, but the risk of moving during the procedure may worsen the situation. It's more expensive but I prefer safety, especially as I will be asleep for the nose surgery.

For nasal reconstruction, we start with breaking everything. When I say break, it's breaking! We open the nasal septum at the bottom of the nose to access the bone, we take a hammer and a chisel and break it to the top. The bones once broken are reduced and then repositioned, it will be necessary to wait 6 months for them to be fixed again correctly.

It looks like a butcher's shop, everything in less than a square inch and without any visible scars. These doctors, beyond their surgical skills, are true artists. For the face, the final result is visible after six months, it will take a year for the nose. The doctor must assume the appearance that it will have in the future ... As for sex change, not only the aspect is more realistic but in addition it is functional. Bravo to the artists!

An appointment is made for the next day at the hospital, this time I will only stay one night, the convalescence will be in my hotel room.

Dr. Burin wants to take advantage of my presence to see me, I'm in the waiting room, anyway, I have nothing else to do today.

Two girls are sitting in front of me, in their twenties, sexy girls, they are Filipino. Tiny shorts tight between the cheeks, a vertiginous neckline without bra, breasts visible almost every movement, that's not the image of a woman, even a prostitute in the middle of work would not dress like that. One of them asks me why I'm here, I explain her the two coming surgeries and those I had three months ago. I can see that they have gone through the same stages. Without the least complex, they show me their "new" breasts, disproportionate boobs at to the horizontal and rigid.

- *You can touch, no problem ...*

It's horrible, hard, we feel the edges of the silicone implants. When they learn that mine are natural, they dip their hands in my bra to check ... not so unpleasant!

Now comes the lower part but this time with photos, they were operated on 5 months ago but healing seems difficult, the appearance is frankly horrible. At this moment, I really appreciate my luck. The surgeon imposes to have no sex the first three months, an assumption that I would not have even considered. For the Philippines, the operations were paid by their respective lovers, married men having a good situation and maintaining their mistresses. They have been sent back both to be examined, they are obviously eager to enjoy their investment. I treated them as prostitutes, now I pity them, just meat to consume, an investment!

When they see the picture of my female sex after only three months, they are devastated, if only I could do something, get them out of it. Yet they are happy, convinced of being privileged, what a difference of culture.

Dr. Burin is doing his exam with the same thoroughness as usual, speculum and depth measurement, everything is fine, I am good for the service. I did not talk about my orgasm, probably a misplaced embarrassment.

The clinic has changed hospitals for all its surgeries, this one is even more modern, much bigger, more luxurious. For these surgeries, no need to empty the intestines, just to be fasting. I barely have time to put on my hospital blouse when they take me to the surgery block.

I recognize my anesthesiologist :

- *Hello Céline, how are you?*

Great but it's up to you to ask, I'm going to sleep, you have to work ...

A little humor on the operating table does not hurt. As for the previous surgery, not the slightest stress, I am so confident.

The awakening is much easier, the anesthesia was much shorter, three hours instead of six and a half hours. I cannot breathe through my nose, I was warned, it is filled with gas to keep bones in place

During the next 24 hours, I will breathe only by the mouth. Well try, it's much more complicated than it seems. Drinking or eating is difficult. A mask of plaster covers my nose, forehead and cheeks, I feel a very small bandage at the level of the Adam's apple. This mask, I will have to wear it for 8 days permanently and then every night for a month. The price to pay for a nose that does not take up all the space on the face.

The next day after breakfast, Dr. Sutin comes to my rescue. He removes the two yards of gauze that fill my nose, finally I breathe. No worries during the surgery, everything went as planned. He also removes the bandage from the Adam's apple, the scar is barely visible and the outgrowth has disappeared.

I spend a few days in my room to recover, it is not painful but you have to be very careful, the slightest impact would move the nose. That's why we stay on the spot the first week. The Adam's apple clears well. I cannot be betrayed by this ugly bump anymore. Everything I had planned is done, apart from the hair implants. To say that it was the initial project, we will see later ...

After a week, I come back to Hanoi, go back to work very quickly, no pain but my nose is still swollen and sensitive to the touch. It takes time, it's fine, I have all my time.

The dilations become more and more often moments of pleasure. Because of anti-androgens, the libido had completely disappeared for two years. This pleasure, completely unexpected, is a woman's pleasure, so different. In trying to tame my new sex, I discovered that pleasure comes from either the vagina or clitoris. Not only is this pleasure tenfold but in addition, I now have two different sources of pleasure. The idea of "inaugurating" it with a so-called natural dilatation is more and more present.

The problem is, the big problem, I have never been attracted to men, being a woman has not changed that. I still pass an announcement with a photo on a dating website:

- *Mature woman seeks shared pleasure in respect of each.*

In one day, more than 40 responses ... Incredible, I never thought I could attract men! As often, many answers are to be discarded. The majority come from young men wanting to "get a milf". No problem, I posted the ad for that. Looking at their photos, you have to imagine that this person is going to touch you. The over forty years old, I could not do it, I'm crazy, I'm over 50 and I'm looking for young men.

I sympathize with a young Frenchman, 28 years old, not vulgar in his remarks. By honesty I explain my situation, my transition, my pseudo virginity ... everything.

- *No problem, it suits me!*

I'm honestly surprised, many men would refuse knowing that the vagina is essentially created with the penis, the surgeon almost reuse everything ... It amounts to touching what was a male sex before ... disgusting for some!

We make an appointment, he will come tonight! An excitement mixed with stress, what should I wear? and if it does not fit? and if it hurts?

It rings, he's there, I cannot go back, I'll open. I'm wearing a little black dress with lace top, a sexy panty and no bra. He brings a bottle of white wine, makes me a kiss and we sit on the couch. Everything corresponds to his description including his picture. I am surprised to be comfortable and yet I live this scene for the first time, what should I do?

He is very gentle, caresses me slowly, kisses me and suggests that we put ourselves at ease in the room. No way back, we climb the stairs, I'm hot, very hot.

With just as much gentleness, he undresses me, caresses me, I feel so much woman, it's so nice, I let myself go, I surrender.

Three orgasms for the first time, it's just amazing, my body has spasms in all directions that make him laugh. Happy the man who made a woman enjoy three times, he is the king of the world. I savor this moment, I examine the situation, I lie there, a man at my side. Three and a half months ago I was still a man.

CHAPTER 18

THIS MEMORY OF MY FIRST EXPERIENCE IS OMNIPRESENT. I meet other men with more or less success. I discover what is a micropenis, meeting Vietnamese, they are so excited, probably the first time with a Western woman, they do not take more than a few seconds, hello and goodbye...

I try an experiment with a woman, it's a first for her too. These moments are very tender, full of sweetness, fervor but something is missing, I feel that this is not the direction I will take.

No, gentlemen, what is missing is not what you have between your legs. I discover that I really feel like a woman when I'm in the arms of a man. Apart from the first meeting, I do not mention who I was before, I'm just a woman like the others. Men consider me as such, thank you Dr. Burin. No need to go in details, even very close, nobody sees that it is a neo vagina ... Good, that's exactly what I wanted: to be transparent. During sex I appreciate to see me in this passive position, I savor that the man doesn't see who I was before, I am a woman and I finally enjoy the physical pleasure that it provides.

In the space of a few days, two absolutely unexpected things fell on me. I did not imagine for one moment that I could experience pleasure, nor did I imagine for a moment that I could please.

When I did the spring cleaning in my dressing room, I threw all the sexy lingerie thinking that it would never serve, what an idiot! I will have to buy it all again but I'm ready to make this effort.

This is not to congratulate myself but how many men find me beautiful, I really struggled to get used to the idea that I might be desirable. All this is beyond my expectations.

I discover something else and not least: I know exactly what men like. All that I have not received as a man, I can now give it, the effect is immediate, incredible. It looks like a fusion, I know exactly what he feels at this moment, I know the gesture he would like to receive and at the same time, I surrender to my own pleasure. I look at myself: how could I have imagined finding myself in this position so feminine a few months ago?

At my age, I have a young woman's breasts and a narrow vagina that obviously gives a lot of pleasure... I'm learning to control mine, tame it and let loose when it's necessary.

My voice is now stable, feminine, absolutely nothing to hide, I even learn to control it during the moments of pleasure, I did not imagine being so "noisy". If at the moment of enjoying, it's the big trucker's rant coming out of my throat, you can imagine the effect.

I continue to see Tiphaine, more distantly. We work more on difficult situations such as noise, anger, fear or pleasure. We exchange more and more, she becomes a kind of confidante, I have all confidence in her, moreover, she has done a great job.

Laetitia my psychiatrist returned to France just before my surgeries, she saw Celine only in photos, we continue to exchange by email from time to time. I owe her so much.

We're at mid-September, it's been two weeks since I came back from Bangkok, I did so many things in two weeks, incredible.

It's time to calm down, I'm leaving for a show in Nuremberg, Germany, it's the essential meeting point for Palm, one of the two shareholders of the factory. There are no particular reasons for me to go but it allows to make a stop in France and still meet some customers.

I am still lucky to be able to arrange my time almost as I please, to travel in very good conditions, it is a great luxury that I appreciate at its true value.

As usual, I land in Frankfurt, today I booked a ... Maserati Ghibli. The car is beautiful, the trident makes a good impression on the front grille. Everything is perfect until you press the start button. I was expecting a good purr, exhaust pipes spitting ... no, what a horror, a diesel. Even if the sound of diesel is vaguely hidden by a sound of V8, it's really a disappointment. Next step is to propose a Ferrari with diesel?

This does not prevent me from leaving anyway. The interior looks good but nothing more, the Mercedes have nothing to envy, very average for a car of this price, it must be the trident that costs so much or the watch of the dashboard. I accelerate, it goes up slowly, a snail, painfully it reaches 200 km / h, never again this car.

After crossing the Rhine, I make a small detour to buy a fresh baguette and some croissants to have breakfast with my parents. It's really a party to go home, I'm so happy to see them when I ignored them so long.

This time I rented an apartment for four nights, it gives me more independence and I enjoy more the time with Anais. She is happy to see me, Annie has a smile, everything is fine. I took advantage of the weekend with Anaïs and I have two more days to go shopping, it was an absolute necessity, I have nothing to wear.

I leave early in the morning for Nuremberg, a four-and-a-half-hour drive, I do not intend to drive fast even if there are no speed limitations. Incredible as I became so reasonable. Like any driver, I consider myself a good driver... try to find a man who tells you he is a bad driver...

However, I never had any fines, I never speeded or lost points or blew into the balloon, sorry, the breathalyzer.

After more than four hours of driving, I find the Nuremberg Exhibition Park, in fact, the GPS finds it, but how was it done before?

I wear tightly fitting black pants, a white silk blouse with long sleeves, black pumps and a down jacket with fur. I like this outfit, I feel good.

I walk through the doors of the exhibition, I feel the eyes of males on me, the beginning of my breast is clearly visible, I savor ... Andy has his stand in front of the entrance, one of the best locations, he must have about 100 m^2. The Palm staff is easily identifiable with their T-shirts, many customers circulate around the alleys. All these products come out of the Hanoi factory, a certain pride, I take photos, all workers must see this.

I walk in the bays, the men look at me and smile at me, I think first of all that we know each other but no, it is to the woman that they smile. It is a very new sensation to feel the gaze of men. Should we rejoice to be watched, even desired? In my case, clearly yes, it's just very nice.

I see old Chinese colleagues, they have not changed, I did change, nobody recognizes me... I call them by their first name and speak to them in Chinese ... they understand ... They have their mouth wide open and look at me from head to toe. Too funny to see them that way. They need to take pictures, nobody would believe them when they come back. I stand a head higher than them but never mind. I'm really happy to see them again, we talk about our respective paths during these few years and we exchange our emails.

A few more steps and here I am face to face with Robert, he did bad things on my back, I should thank him today. He does not recognize me of course, I talk to him, he looks at me, he just understood, he literally falls into his chair and takes his head in his hands

- *It's you, is it you? How is it possible?*

He really struggles to take the hit, I tell my story but I do not go too far, too many bad things happened even if I do not have any bitterness today.

For those who know professional shows, the most difficult is not to meet customers during the day, the hardest begins at the time of closing. Each stand comes out bottles of wine, beer, canapés or other specialties. We move from one booth to another, each puts his own music, we drink again and again. I keep the mind clear, I drink only water but for others, the alcohol helping, I start to be flirted. Still something new, how to react to that, I slap him?

Not really an option, Bob is Andy's partner, I will stay calm. It's amazing how many situations you have to adjust in a matter of seconds. As I said, there is no manual that explains how to be a woman overnight.

The evening continues in the restaurant, Bob becomes more and more insistent ... I keep smiling but I do not imagine this man over 60 years old will touch me. He asks me my room number that he will not get, anyway, with the alcohol he has in his blood, he could not even remember the number.

I'm in my hotel room, alone, I smile looking at myself in the mirror, only new experiences today. Tomorrow, I'm leaving for Hanoi.

CHAPTER 19

I STILL ENJOY MY WORK AT THE FACTORY, especially since my outfits have completely changed. The girls in the office always dress elegantly, feminine and refined. When I go up the stairs and along the corridor that leads to my office, I feel all these eyes on me, an inspection in order.

I pay close attention to what I wear, always coordinated. Sometimes cross-legged, sometimes in jeans but always feminine. To my surprise, the wearing of jeans does not prevent femininity or even being classy.

If they inspect me this way, it's to check if I have not made any mistakes. If that happened, they would come immediately to advise me, to suggest to me something else, real mother hens.

I go through the workshop, my heels hit the tiles, this sound sounds like a love song. Six months ago, I did not imagine showing myself that way.

I was afraid of losing part of my authority, it is not so, on the contrary. I have earned the respect and admiration of many of them. Without wanting to, I prepared the ground very well, no surprise. The whole factory floats on a small cloud, everything works, everything rolls, it's just magic.

Mike comes to Hanoi with a future client, Troy, whom we met in Salt Lake City. He offers a promising and completely new product on the market. We had a very good contact, a very enthusiastic guy who specializes in big game fishing in Florida. Of course, I did not talk about my story: for him, I am a woman, this is how.

I make him visit the factory, he is impressed and excited about the possibilities ahead. Of course, we talk about fishing, I can talk to him about my catches but I cannot show pictures, it is a man who keeps the fish. Mike shows his photos with tuna caught in Tokyo Bay. He then has the good idea to show the next picture:

- *Do you know this guy?*

Of course, Troy does not recognize me

- *It's her!*

It takes some time to react and this very positively, he has a friend who has followed the same course. I'm in a though rage, if I want to talk about it, it's up to me to do it, no one else. It's like belonging to Freemasonry, I'm free to declare myself, but in no case would I speak of a brother or a sister. I catch Mike, calmly I explained to him my anger, he does not have to do this stuff.

Later, I continue to browse Tinder for possible encounters. I am so surprised by the vulgarity of a majority of men. Are women attracted by this kind of attitude? I have a hard time believing it.

At this stage, I do not know my sexual identity, no importance, it is time that will decide it according to different experiences.

I go on a weekend in Hoi An. I love this city in the center of Vietnam, former capital, beautiful period houses and many pedestrian streets. I do not go alone, Anh accompanies me, I am the first surprised. She is my age, married, her husband is no longer interested in her, something quite normal in Vietnam. Long black hair, fleshier than the majority of Vietnamese, I have a natural attraction for her, but I never told her anything.

At the weekend, I give swimming lessons to girls in the office and from my gym, none can swim, Anh is one of them. Curiously they tell me it is safe now. It's more the rumors that cause the most problems, a woman who teaches a woman does not cause any problem. On a Saturday, under the pretext of swimming lessons, we kiss in the pool and then we continue more comfortably. This is her first experience with a woman, I do not know if she sees the woman in me or the previous man. The pleasure is at the rendezvous but in a very different way, I give you then you give me. With a man, the pleasure is shared, at the same time, another discovery.

The weekend is frankly difficult, I'm not used to share my bed, I appreciate so much my loneliness, I do not really feel ready to share this bed.

In addition to having an alternating pleasure, I find myself in the old male-female pattern. I know now that a relationship of this type will not suit me. At the opposite, I still have no attraction for men, a Kafkaesque situation.

Nothing presses, I appreciate each moment of my new life being alone. The upheavals are so fast, which is true today will not be tomorrow.

Come Christmas time, Celine's first, the first big family reunion. My two suitcases are full of Vietnamese gifts, crafts, tea, dishes, lacquers...

I take my usual flight, Hanoi -Bangkok-Frankfurt. My car is functional, too much luggage to rent a sports car, I'm happy with a BMW X5.

I rent an apartment in the city center for Anaïs and I, we both appreciate so much this time to meet. We are planning a dinner with Annie again, which makes Anaïs so happy.

The Christmas holidays usually happen at my parents' house, we are all together on the 24th or the 25th. It will also be the first Christmas without Jeannette, the first in 21 years.

My two sisters, their husbands, their children, a table of 13, nobody is superstitious. Aperitif then distribution of gifts, from the youngest to the oldest. These gifts are always customized to the image of the one who receives them. For the first time, I unpack perfume, beauty creams, jewelry, every minute is lived fully.

The children are delighted, especially Daphne, Stephanie's daughter, my other sister: I offered her a box of makeup.

- *Auntie... Auntie...?*

Daphne repeats it several times, nobody reacts. Heck, Auntie it's me, nobody had caught it, giggles all around. Laetitia, my psychologist, was formal: the acceptance of children is almost immediate, no social barrier hinders them.

Come the moment of the photos, Céline will make her first appearance with all her family around. There is nothing stronger than I can wish for anyone starting the same course.

Collective photos then the one I was waiting for: the three sisters together. Seeing me on all these pictures happy, radiant, it's so hard to believe.

The meal is still appreciated, Mom is an outstanding cook. What good times, I do not remember having spent better with family:

I would like to thank everyone for the place you have made for Céline.

It's said, several times I wanted to start my sentence but the tears came, I had to say it ... The holidays extend over three days. Alsace benefits from December 26 and Easter Friday as additional days of leave compared to the rest of France, heritage of the German period.

I offered a new Samsung tablet to Anaïs that she keeps close to her, it is fantastic and has all the qualities. As expected, we go out for dinner with Annie in a very small charming restaurant.

Anaïs understood well that she shouldn't call me Dad outside, she calls me Celine, Annie does the same, the first time, what a surprise!

I made peace with myself, I removed a heavy weight from my shoulders.

The separation is 25 years old but we have always kept a good contact, it has never been so good as today.

We order, the dishes are really excellent, we discuss everything and nothing when she says:

I just realized that everyone sees you as a woman, I did not understand before.

Oops, what emotions for the same evening. Anaïs is happy and fulfilled, I have never felt so well, it is normal that this well-being transpires. She smiles as I have never seen her smile, a moment of shared happiness ... They are so rare.

My time is short, I absolutely have to be at the factory on December 28th to finalize the tax audit before the end of the accounting year. I do not count the return flights already made, a routine.

A woman of fifty years conducts this audit with two other colleagues. We meet at the scheduled time, Long, my financial manager will take care of the translations.

We made some mistakes that justify a fine, nothing serious, then comes the negotiation to obtain a discharge. We are in Vietnam, corruption exists at all levels, teachers, doctors, customs, police, officials, firefighters ... everywhere.

I had left the previous negotiation to Julien, my right arm. This is a situation where I can lose control and become violent ... verbally. To take the money that the entire factory has generated is just unbearable. Since I'm a woman, my temperament has changed completely, I'm ready to face this woman and corruption:

- *You are very beautiful, you have children?*
- *I have a 26-year-old daughter who works in France*

Incredible, I have a 26-year-old son who works in a bank, do you think they could meet? With such a beautiful mother, your daughter must be beautiful.

Oops, it all takes a funny turn, I cannot tell her that I'm dad. However, the compliments I take them willingly. She comes next to me to sign me tons of documents. Without moving, I see that it is put in position to probe my cleavage ... If it can bring down the bribe, I'm fine to use my body. I refrain from bursting out laughing.

Long who ensures the translation is red peony and no longer knows where to put himself, she is all against me. During the signatures, our hands brush against each other, I feel her breathing faster, she sticks to my chair ... What a sensation of power, I like it!

We have nothing to pay, incredible, Julien had escaped with $ 65,000 for customs. I'm coming out with a promise of a meal. The power of being a woman, awesome.

A big thorn is removed, I can think of New Year's Eve, the first I will spend abroad and without Jeannette. I want to realize an old fantasy, a naughty evening between two women and a man. I contact Anh who immediately agrees and finds Thinh, a 25-year-old Vietnamese boy.

As a man, watching two women at his side caress is the climax of excitement. Indeed, Thinh was very valiant for several hours, incredible, I was really an average lover when I was a guy.

We had a very nice evening but I still cannot share my bed. It's still incredible, among all these men already met, not one has suspected anything. I honestly did a cross on sex, who would want a 53-year-old trans woman?

On January 3rd, I consult my emails, First Instance Court of Nantes... An adrenaline discharge, by clicking I will discover perhaps that I am officially a woman.

We regret to inform you that the court of Nantes is not competent for expatriates, you should contact the First Instance Court of Colmar.

What, it is more than six months since I filed my request and I am informed today that they are not competent. I cannot believe it, rabies invades me, I sent three letters explaining all the humiliations, bullying, identity checks that I had to undergo at immigration of several countries (I never had to suffer the slightest humiliation, I'm just trying to accelerate the process). After all these letters, they tell me that they are not competent? I cannot let that go, I have to do something. The only possible action is the appeal to the High Council of Magistracy. My request for non-assistance to person at risk is sent on January 10, to date, more than a year later, not the slightest response. Is this the justice of our country? The all-powerful judges have all the rights and when an appeal is filed, we are not even listened to, I am disgusted.

I have no choice but to turn to the first instance court of Colmar. I contact Ms Huber, lawyer, who was recommended to me. I settle the agreement and she immediately takes the file in charge. I would not have needed to use a lawyer but it facilitates and especially speeds up the processing of the case.

A few days later, I receive an email from her:

The next first instance court hearing will be held on Thursday, January 25, 2018. I am waiting for the notice of hearing to communicate it to you. I would like to tell you that your presence is essential, since the president has indicated that videoconferencing is not possible.

Heck, another 20,000 km to go, I had not planned to return to France so quickly. One thing is certain, I cannot miss this opportunity. I do not quite understand their reasoning, my name is feminine, my genes are feminine, my sex too. Do they need to see me in person to make their decision?

CHAPTER 20

FORTUNATELY, I have never had anything to do with justice, I understood that all discussion is useless.

I take my ticket, I arrive in Frankfurt, I take a Shelby, my Ford Mustang GT, breakfast at my parents. In twelve years of expatriation, they have never seen me so much.

Later in the morning, I sit on the bench, I meet my lawyer for the first time, nothing special to add to the record. We will go last, probably one to two hours of waiting. I am surprised calm, relaxed, I have no doubt about the outcome of the hearing.

The sessions are held in camera for reasons of confidentiality, all cases affect the family in general. It's my turn, a big wooden room, absolutely nobody on the benches, 3 judges at the top of a platform, the prosecutor, a clerk and my lawyer.

I am placed in the middle, crushed by this impressive decorum. The height of the judges and the prosecutor speaks volumes about the value of the litigant. What a terrible game of intimidation! Learning in Freemasonry, classes in lecture halls full of students, speeches to my employees helped me through this ordeal.

Dad, you're so beautiful

- *Mister Céline Audebeau, please explain the reason for your presence?*
- *Well, the first reason is not to make me call Mister anymore!*

I develop all my history, from childhood to today, the surgeries practiced, the difficulties to immigration. For 15 minutes, the three women magistrates and the prosecutor listen to me without interrupting me.

The President speaks:

- *Mr. Prosecutor, what do you think of a decision taken on the seat?*

But what are they talking about, what is this seat? The prosecutor speaks:

- *Miss. Audebeau, can you remind me of your profession?*
- *I am General Manager of a factory in Hanoi and member of the board of directors of a Japanese company.*

Theatrically, he raises his arms to heaven:

- *Obviously, Madam President, I agree with a decision on the seat.*

Solemnly, the president speaks to me:

- *Ms. Audebeau, we confirm the gender change in your birth certificate.*
- Thank you, Madam President.
- *Are you going to stay a little here to enjoy this beautiful sun?*
- *For sure not Madam President, I made 20 thousand kilometers just to meet you.*

I managed to make a court of law laugh. As of this day, this time, I am officially female, Yessssssss!

My lawyer shows me the exit, we leave this impressive room:

- *Do you realize what just happened? she asks me*
- *Yes, they agree with my request*
- *Yes, but a decision on the seat, do you realize?*
- *Absolutely not, what is it?*
- *They made the decision immediately, no deliberations, in 26 years of career, I never saw that!*
- *Oh ...*
- *You were so convincing, I had nothing more to say!*

Not only am I a woman but I get it in an exceptional way. The same evening, the judgment was pronounced:

The court ruling on gracious matters and at first instance:

- *SAYS that Céline Audebeau, male, born.... From now on, Céline Audebeau being female...*

I have the judgment, my grail, here I am officially female, I have to read and re-read it to believe it. Thanks to Olivia and all those activists who fought. We still need to go through the first instance court but the procedure has been reduced by this simplification law.

Vietnam passed a law on 1 January 2017 allowing gender change in administrative documents. It is the first country in Asia to pass a law for transgender people. Thailand does not have any such laws as the country has the largest number of transgender people.

It is just unacceptable that in France, the country of human rights, it is still necessary to ask permission from a psychiatrist to freely dispose of one's body! I did not use this authorization simply because my financial resources allowed me to ignore it, it's even worse, everyone should have the same opportunities.

Who can still accept that nowadays? The brakes of our dear decision makers are very diverse, prudishness, all those who were against marriage for all do not have enough open mind to listen to the demands of transgender people.

Then, even if parity is inscribed in our constitution, we are still in a phallocratic society, the power of the dominant male.

Finally, the law is not yet very clear. It is not necessary to go through the surgery or sterilization to change gender in the civil registry. Ultimately, this woman can become a child's dad ... lots of complicated situations. In no case should the right alone prevent a person from living in accordance with one's self.

CHAPTER 21

ANOTHER SCARY event is the big annual factory party for the arrival of Tet, the equivalent of the Chinese New Year. This is the biggest festival of the year for the Vietnamese, the plant will close for 10 days. But before that, we organize a big party: the 420 collaborators in the same room for a meal, a show and an important lottery.

As General Director, of course I have to make my speech to open the ceremony. This will be Celine's first speech, what anguish. Not related to the number of people but they will hear my voice for the first time. I am anxious about the emotion that I will have to control.

I prepare my speech, I describe the activity of the last twelve months, prospects for the future, I thank everyone for their seriousness, not a single container on the 243 shipped was late. As a result, we realize the highest profit since the 10 years of existence of the factory. Part of this profit will be distributed to employees. As in China, many factories lose 10% to 15% or more of its employees who do not return after the new year. It's been five years in a row that 100% of employees have returned, it's just amazing. Working conditions must not be so painful but what makes the difference is that they feel respected.

I polish my speech and finish with a personal note, it's still not trivial that the male boss becomes a female boss.

- *... a small personal note to finish, I am very happy to be like that front of you. 2017 will remain the most important year of my life. I want to thank each of you for the way you welcomed me. I am very lucky to work with you and to live in Vietnam...*

At the moment when I write it and when I read it again, the throat tightens, the eyes become wet, the voice changes ... I must not crack, I read and re-read while trying to control my emotions. Not that easy!

Hang comes home to help me choose my outfit, I have different skirts or dresses that would do the trick, one is a long dress specially purchased for this occasion. Celine has never worn it, yet the closet overflows. Hang suggests I keep it for the 10-year ceremony in May. This will be a black straight skirt topped with a white silk blouse and black pumps with heels. After stopping smoking, the kilos have accumulated, I will really have to do something. I also see the chance to fall flat on my face by going up on the stage with my heels... as if I needed extra pressure.

I have to be there at 11:30am, I go to the beauty salon Miss Nhi, she is waiting me for a makeup. When a pro makes you up, the result is so different, yet it seems that I proceed in the same way.

Arriving in front of the banquet room, as usual, all the staff is already sitting, I have to make my entrance from the back, everyone gets up to applaud. Frankly, there is absolutely nothing spontaneous in this attitude, we are in a communist country where to applaud a leader is part of the folklore. This year is however different, all eyes are focused on me, many smiles on me ... the pressure rises.

Two masters of ceremony are at work, one for Vietnamese, the other for English. Miss Céline is called for her speech ...

I trained, I read and reread this last passage, it should pass, I am confident. Ten minutes of numbers, thanks, perspectives, I arrive at my text.

No worries, everything happens as in training, I finish my sentence:

- *... I am very lucky to work with you and live in Vietnam ... Cam on (thanks)*

I did not crack, excellent! At these last words, they all get up to applaud me, sincerely this time ... Damn, I was so well prepared, the tears come at a crazy speed. After all, you have to stop wanting to control your emotions at all costs and just enjoy this magical moment. Several people come on stage to offer me flowers, hug me and of course take a picture, what a strong moment!

I can finally get back to my seat, so many emotions but I'm so happy. This moment that it was impossible for me to imagine right after my operations has become a moment that I will not forget. The party ends at 4:00pm, my arms are filled with flowers, I am a poor woman to complain about.

I come home, collapse on the couch, I cry, so much pressure, joy, happiness, a feeling of fullness.

Finally, the time of New Year's holidays, my ticket for Phuket Thailand is in my possession for several weeks. I was hoping to occupy my villa but it is the very high season. It is better to rent it and pay the hotel.

Phuket is the pearl of Asia, an island south an hour's flight from Bangkok. There are all the features of Thailand, small islands and beautiful beaches, excellent street restaurants, fishing villages, family areas and finally Patong Beach, sex to the extreme. Even if you have to drive to the left, I am very comfortable to ride motorbikes or cars, usually I rent both.

This time, none of that, no car, no motorbike, I stay there ... in Patong. In the day, everything is calm, hard to imagine what will happen a few hours later. I came on vacation with Jeannette a few years ago. My hotel is right next to one of the biggest shopping centers on the island. I know in advance that my suitcase will quickly overflow.

My room is relatively ordinary, it looks directly on the pool as I requested.

I quickly unpack my suitcase to find my bikini, my beach dress and my hat. If there's one thing I hate, it's crowded beaches. For several years, I have been staying in extremely quiet hotels, Jeannette and I were often the only ones on the beach. This time it is very different, it is a test that I impose myself, to produce myself in public in swimsuit.

I cross the Bangla Road, one of the hottest streets in Thailand. At this time, only a few bars are open offering fresh beers for less than one buck. The beach is there, I opt for sunbeds, too bad to pay something but I prefer to be in the shade. If I bronze, the scars of the face would become very visible.

In a bikini, sunglasses on the nose, I feel so good, that's it, I'm there ... You have to assume. I go back and forth between my sunbed and the sea. When I go back to the water for the fifth time, a French couple walked on the beach. She cannot help saying to her husband:

- *Look, he's a guy.*

Viewed from behind with my shoulders and my size, it's only half astonishing. I did not react to her comment, I'm not going to give them that pleasure, I just returned slightly, looking like she could see me from the front.

- *Oh no, she's a girl.*

Seeing the breasts and especially the bottom without hump, she changed her mind, hiding a willy in a bikini is rather difficult. I tried when I was in Koh Samui, you should not spread your legs otherwise ... But that I'm stupid, why do I need to justify myself for this woman who should rather worry at the size of her buttocks?

Since my surgery, I travelled in Thailand, Vietnam, USA, Germany, Netherland, China, Japan, Korea and Norway. It's only in from French people that I heard that kind of comments showing that tolerance is quite poor compared to the other countries. Sad!

My passing exam is successful, I merged in the mass. On these beaches, the mass there is, incredible as it hangs everywhere, especially the Russians. I have no complex to have, which reassures me frankly.

I do not want to stay in the sun too long, the heat becomes heavy and I finished my book. A good improvised nap took me a good part of the afternoon.

For the evening meal, I spotted a seafood restaurant where ladyboys are serving. I do not search for them precisely but for once they can do something other than prostitute or masseuse,

I feel obliged to support them. The meal is very good, they are very nice and try to discuss.

It's just odious to see the behavior of men towards them, for them, they are neither women nor men, for them everything is allowed. I would like to get up and slap them one by one. It must be said that in this kind of place, do not expect an intellectual elite, it is closer to the gutter and everything goes under the belt.

On a website, I spotted a massage parlor dedicated to women, I had to try. My masseur must be 25 years old, cute, the massage is perfect until the fateful question:

- *Do you want more service?*

You just have to agree on the price and you get the full service. This sentence I had heard as a man but this is the first time for Celine. After all, a little fun is not going to hurt.

On the way back, I venture into the Bangla road that is swarming with people. A Chinese group cross the street running after a flag, they take a maximum picture of girls moving their body on stages. Old paunchy guys drool in front of the girl who dances right above them. Young gangs who think they are kings of the world, thinking that only their seduction attracts girls. It is in a place like this that we find the primary instinct of the male ... it's just lamentable but it's a show.

The next day, I spend a good part of the day on the beach, I took five books to read for the week, a small salad at noon, a nap and we are already in the evening.

I go back to the same restaurant, first because it was very good but also to see my girlfriends again. The meal is even better than the day before, always the same kind of idiots at certain tables. Yesterday, going to massage, I spotted another shop with girls and some ladyboys. To perform on the beach was my first challenge, the second one to be massaged by a trans, would she see something?

She is really shy, little glasses, a book in hand and behind all the other girls. She has nothing of the girls from the Bangla Road, she seems very discreet. She has no breasts at all, her voice is deep but her features are very soft. The massage is perfect, I have the right to the usual proposal that I accepted. It was very good, very sweet ...

The massage finished, I talk to her about my different operations, which had little interest until now becomes the main subject:

- *In which clinic did you go? who was the surgeon? Why we do not see anything? why you do not have breast implants? ...*

The questions fuse, I do not have time to answer that another arrives. I realize that I made a mistake, in her enthusiasm, she calls her trans girlfriends one by one look carefully at the new jewel that I have between the legs. Second exam passed, she saw nothing.

I chose to spend the second part of the holidays on the island of Ko Yao Noi. It is reached by speed boat in 40 minutes, there is only one road on the island, even a blonde could not get lost. A single 7/Eleven store, absolute tranquility. I booked a bungalow with private pool, I'm not disappointed, I'll cocoon myself for the next few days. Apart from painful dinners with an empty chair front of me, I read, rest, walk, spend time on the deserted beach, just perfect, a real vacation.

Barely two days after this beautiful holiday, Mom and Bénédicte arrive in Hanoi. We will be the three of us, Bénédicte has prepared a busy schedule: between the factory visit, the ceramic village of Bat Trang and Halong Bay. What good times but also lost time: 53 years to vegetate. I waited so long to have a good time with them. Mom discovers everything and for the first time in her life, she gets a massage, she cannot believe how good it is. We walk in the streets of Hoi An, Hanoi, explore some caves and visit temples in Ninh Binh. Their suitcases are full to bursting when they leave. We had such a good time ... between women!

I was very wise during these 10 days with my family. I go back on Tinder and very quickly I get in touch with Matteo, a young Italian of 32 years who travels around the world by bike. He tells me he worked 12 years saving the maximum. He started his journey in Bangkok, India, Nepal, Laos and here he is in Vietnam for a few days, next step Taiwan.

I invite him to eat, which will allow us to get to know one another: he dreams of a pizza. Proposing to make a pizza to an Italian is suicide. I make my own dough, those of the trade do not suit me, I garnish it, a lot of cheese. My pizza has a lot of success, he eats three quarters of it ... I'm his dessert, wow, he is just exceptional, very sweet, very attentive, patient. We go through different places: from the kitchen to the bedroom then the pool and finally the sofa. What endurance, I was really bad next to him ... This evening is just exceptional ...

For the first time, I would like to see a man again and this is the case 10 days later, even stronger and more intense. I know what he feels every moment, I put his hand in the neck and caress, a true symbiosis. I am in his arms, we are exhausted, for the first time I feel good in the arms of a man. His chest hair, his beard does not bother me at all, I feel so much a woman, so happy.

He leaves tomorrow for Taiwan, a pity but who knows, after Taiwan he will go to Japan, we will see maybe. One thing is certain, I now know my sexual orientation.

Dad, you're so beautiful

CHAPTER 22

MARCH 2018, I receive a message inviting me to make an appointment at the embassy to pick up my new passport and my new identity card.

My modified birth certificate states that my name is Celine and I am now a female. Officially, being still married to Jeannette, we are a lesbian couple. Before the adoption of the Marriage for All Act, such a thing would not have been possible, it would have been necessary to divorce before I could ask for gender change.

My new passport, I have it in my hands, I open it feverishly and I direct my eyes directly on the "F" so expected, what emotion, I am finally officially recognized as a woman. Flore, the person in charge of passports at the Embassy sees my emotion well:

- *I am very happy for you ... Madam*

By insisting on this "madam", she is so kind, she did everything to make my life easier for all these administrative procedures. That's it, this passport is the starting point for all other upcoming changes.

Making the changes at the bank is pretty simple but what about the loans that are still running in the name of Christophe? They will stay in the state until they expire.

The change of driving license requires living in France, in theory, you cannot change when you are an expatriate. During a stay in France, I was arrested by the police in the city of Colmar, I was coming back from a meal at my sister's, my daughter was at my side. I drove a BMW M4 have 4 exhausts, you can imagine the sound, the police car blocked me like in movies ... anything!

- *Hello lady, vehicle papers and driver's license.*

I searched in the glove compartment, I quickly found the German documents of the car and I handed my driving license:

- *This is not your driver's license madam!*

No wonder, on the photo, I'm 19 years old with a beard ... well, how to explain to them. I presented them my second passport where my name is Christophe and I am male. I also handed out a document that the Embassy produced explaining that Mr. Christophe and Mrs. Céline are one and the same person. They did not argue ... but I had to blow for the first time in my life... and I did not drink a drop of alcohol.

- *Madam, you drive without light on your vehicle!*

But what a blonde I am, I smile, I did not notice anything. They have not bothered me, I left with the lights this time! Anais was terrified.

- *If they put you in jail, how am I going to do without my dad?*

She was really scared, everything that is uniform scares her a bit.

I still need this driver's license or I will not be able to rent a car anymore. My passport and my credit card are in the name of Céline and the driver's license in the name of Christophe. As an expatriate, it is not possible to apply for a renewal of a driving license in France. I use the address of my parents, as everything is computerized, no verification is performed.

Ironically, I now have two valid passports, one male with Christophe and the other female with Céline ... There are probably few people in the world who have two identities of different sexes and both valid!

Many other things are to change: social security, retirement, taxes, dozens of accounts that you have on all websites, diplomas ... It must first change my social security number, finished the "1" for males 1640668 ... replaced to the "2" 2640668 ...!

The most difficult changes to be made will undoubtedly concern the legal documents of the company in Vietnam. I went to see our lawyer before the surgeries, I explained to him that he will have to deal with a case that he never had before. He laughed saying that he has been working in this branch for over twenty years and that he has certainly seen it all. Well no, he was speechless ... Indeed, it never happened to him, learning, it was never done in Vietnam. There is a law that authorizes gender change in Vietnam but the implementing decree has never passed.

I am a shareholder and legal representative of the company but Christophe cannot sell his shares to Celine who lives at the same address, was born on the same date and has the same bank account.

In addition, as an expatriate, you need to have enough professional experience to be accepted. Céline has no past, no experience and no diplomas at the moment.

The lawyer invokes this law authorizing gender change in immigration services and in the administration that administers business licenses. They recognize that Christophe and Céline are one and the same person and that all the documents will be modified accordingly...

Incredible, it's done, I'm the first person in Vietnam to benefit from gender change as hundreds of Vietnamese women have been waiting for years. This information comes to the ears of the press, the Vietnam News daily contacts me to report on my story. They want to do a press article and a video for TV.

What to do? I just wanted to go unnoticed, that nobody pays attention to me and I am asked to put myself forward. On the other hand, talking about this topic in a national newspaper and on Vietnamese TV would be a huge step forward for this country, I accept.

A team of three journalists arrive in the company, a print journalist, a camerawoman and Paul, an English journalist for the TV report.

I had met Paul in a cafe the week before to rough out the subject and allow them to structure the interview. The first time I was filmed this way, several trips back and forth in the corridors, downstairs to the workshops and then shots in different departments of the factory. Then come the interviews in my office, I introduce myself, I talk about my family, my work, how was my return to the factory, the reception of Vietnamese. I am comfortable ... everything is done in English of course. They also interview some of my colleagues, I do not hear what they say, I'll see it during the broadcast. I then spend a lot of time with the print journalist who asks me hundreds of questions. I reported some photos as they had asked me. Nearly 6 hours of shooting and interviews, I am exhausted and my voice is out of order. It is not really stabilized yet and I really pulled too hard on the vocal cords. Finally, it was a great experience, I am really curious and eager to see the result.

We are in June 2018, the whole factory is travelling to Vinh for what we call the summer holidays, almost seven hours drive. This is an event that I established 6 years ago, every year, the whole factory goes for two or three days by the sea. Many have never seen the ocean and they love to be together. Nine crowded buses, two-thirds are sick and vomit where they can, they are not used to transport. I make it a point to attend even if it does not correspond to the kind of weekend that I appreciate but it is so important for them. Hundreds of photos are taken with the boss, this proximity, I consider it an investment, I share the same things as them, I'm not above.

It is during the way back that the Vietnam News makes its publication. An insert on the first page and an inside double-page, incredible! I find all my photos including those before and after that impress everyone.

The video is available on their website, I hasten to find it. Oh my god, I'm big, I move like an elephant, my voice is not very feminine ... nothing suits me except the message that corresponds to what I expected.

I am tough with myself in this desire for perfection whereas a few months ago, I would never have expected to be like who I am today. I watch the video again, it's better, they included the video of my return to the factory. A year ago, I was a man and today we film the woman I became, when we see the course, we must learn to be happy.

The Vietnam News is a daily newspaper in English, the impact is relatively limited, only those who speak the language access the website. However, the comments fuse, I receive only messages of admiration and encouragement. I am recognized in the street, I make selfies and I shake hands, incredible. The pages of the newspaper are displayed in the canteen, everyone throws themselves to see the photos of the boss. They know of course who I was before, I see only smiles on their faces, some hug me in their arms, too moving.

CHAPTER 23

SO FAR, I HAVE NEVER HAD A FACEBOOK ACCOUNT, simply because I had nothing to share and I found it rather ridiculous to unpack all its activity. Today, everything has changed, I testify, I exchange, I share, I advise, I learn ... I joined several transgender groups where I discover the stories of others. Most evoke this terrible obstacle course, the dictates of doctors, especially psychiatrists.

Some of these psychiatrists issue the certificate after one or two consultations, most require one to two years of psychotherapy. For most of us, we have this syndrome since our childhood but these doctors still impose two years of psychotherapy to be really sure of our choice ...

The endocrinologist who takes over will not deliver any treatment without a certificate from the psychiatrist. Where is it written? They just have a terrible fear of medical error! There is no law, no regulation, it is just the doctors between them who decide how to proceed ... It scandalizes me to the highest point, you really have to make things happen. I was able to make my transition as I wanted it just because I was able to pay, it's really not normal.

On one of these pages, I find a casting for people who have or are going to change their sex for a France2 show, "it starts today" (first public channel in France). I don't know that TV show, TV5 world is the only French speaking channel that we receive abroad. I really want to testify, I write an introductory email to the reporter. The same day, she asks to contact me by phone to discuss more, her name is Elise.

We discuss for an hour and a half, my childhood, my career, my job, my parents... She is enthusiastic, my story interests her a lot, she will submit it to the editor the next day.

Barely three days after having sent my first email, the editorial office confirms that my application has been considered. The show will be recorded at the end of July at Réservoir Prod studios in Paris. In the process, I take my ticket, the recording of the show is a Friday, I will stay the weekend to enjoy Paris. It is a great luxury to have flexibility in my agenda.

I take my regular airline company to arrive in Paris. I booked a hotel room in the Saint-Germain-des-Prés district, I really wanted to go back to the Orsay museum and take a tour of the Louvre. The room is shabby, a shame, nothing to do with the photos of the website, a room all in length where it is impossible to go on both sides of the bed. I hate being cheated that way, is that how we welcome the 90 million visitors each year in France? A shame, nothing to do, they will take one of these remarks on Booking, they can trust me for that.

I sit on my bed, the TV is high, it is 2:00pm, it would be good to watch at least once the show I will attend tomorrow. Faustine Bollaert is the journalist presenting the show, she leads the debate perfectly and each person is respected, it seems pretty good. At the same time, it is quite unreal to say that tomorrow I will be on this TV studio.

At lunch time, I move to the cafe Flore, a mythical place right in front of the hotel! I still do not know how to dress for the shooting, a dress, a skirt, pants? I decide to do my own survey, I count the women who pass by me and I note the way they are dressed. We are in July, it's hot, 97 women out of 100 are wearing pants... so it will be pants. Returning to the hotel, I consult "my Facebook", I added some photos and comments. I also discovered another call to witness for TF1 this time (first private channel TV in France), the subject is "I changed sex". As before, I answer, we'll see.

Filming for France2 is scheduled for 1:00pm but they ask that we be present well in advance. A driver looks for me at 9:30 and drives me to the studios. Elise, whose voice I only know, is waiting for me on the landing, she makes me cross the various security checks. The show has a studio audience, which adds a little tension.

A shoot is underway on a very hard subject, "my husband or child died during my delivery" really nothing funny and we feel the tension among all the staff outside the studio.

Elise takes me to an empty studio so that we can see how to frame my testimony together.

- *I did not tell you but you will be the main guest, half of the show will be dedicated to you.*

Oops, I was not expecting that ... No worries, I'm ready. The subject has really been very worked, everything is documented, argued, we review step by step the elements of my testimony, there is still time to delete or add things, it's really nice to be consulted in this way before the show begins. She checks especially with me if I agree that Faustine asks me my old male name. It's part of my story, even if I start a new life, there's no reason to deny the old one.

We agree on all points, everything is clear and I feel really confident. I am then driven to a small room where the other participants of the show are gathered. Jonas is a handsome young man who has been the mother of a little girl, the transformation is impressive. Victorine has just started her transition, it's the beginning, she has not yet feminine traits even if she feels like a woman for a long time. Maxence is still in his teens, he is accompanied by Claire his mother, we feel a lot of weight, heaviness between them. We quickly get to know each other around sandwiches that will serve as a midday meal.

Comes the time to go to makeup and hairstyle, like real stars. Watching all this behind the scenes has something thrilling ... I'm ready, my pink salmon pants and my little black sweater with a deep neckline satisfy me, I think I made the right choice. I would not want to give another image, not to show a woman who pushes femininity to the extreme, I just want to be a woman like the others, that's part of my message.

The time comes to settle in the studio, exactly what I saw yesterday on TV, funny impression. The audience is already installed and they applaud, a lump in my throat. I'm the first on the bench, just sitting next to Faustine. She arrives a few minutes before the start of the show, she kisses us, reassures us, explains the course ... in fact, it really puts us at ease. The show starts!

As expected, Faustine interrogates me first, in front of me is Dr. Machefaux, a psychiatrist specializing in gender dysphoria.

Faustine launches the debate, she asks the first questions and I start, it's amazing how comfortable I feel, the words come out quickly, I can't stop. I was able to express my rejection of psychiatrists, because they can decide for me whether or not I can dispose of my body as I understand it. At one point, when I talk about surgeries, Faustine tells me I'm beautiful. If I had thought one day that I could be told that I'm beautiful, I would never have believed it, today it's happening in front of the cameras.

I speak more than thirty minutes and I could still continue but Jonas, Victorine and Maxence also have things to say. At the end of the show, Faustine, who was great clairvoyance and who led the discussion beautifully comes to me:

- *Celine, throughout the show, I was destabilized by your eyes, your eyes express so much.*

All this while making me a warm kiss, I'm just happy. I was able to express what I had to say about my daughter, my parents, my sisters, my colleagues and psychiatrists. It was well worth it.

The recording lasted a little over an hour but I'm fried, exhausted nervously, it's still not commonplace to end up on a television set of a prime time show. Elise informs me that it will be broadcast in two to three months, there is still more waiting!

Leaving the recording studio, we are all on a terrace, special links are established between us, we are so close to each other. Leaving the building, the public is still there, I have many congratulations, many admire me ... it's too much ... I am delighted to find my shabby hotel room to rest... so many emotions!

Emotions, I'm not at the end, looking at my emails, I discovered that the journalist of TF1 would like us to meet tomorrow to talk about the subject ... I suddenly feel like being on another planet, I just finish the TV shoot for France2, now TF1 is also interested in my profile ... Be careful not to lose control and all this does not climb to my head

The journalist is called Carole, we agree to a meeting Saturday afternoon at 2:00 near Pigalle.

I take the morning to visit the Orsay Museum, I enjoy watching the works of my favorite artist: Degas. The visit ended, I take the subway to eat a piece near Montmartre, I will not be far from my appointment.

It's almost 2:00pm, I'm sitting on the terrace of a shadowy cafe sipping lemon juice. Carole arrives on time, she alone can recognize me thanks to the photos that I sent her. She sees me from afar, seeing her look at me, I discover it. In her forties, she smiles broadly as she sits down, and is an associate editor at TF1. The show she is responsible for will be 90 minutes on the theme "I changed sex", it will be broadcast on TFX prime time and TF1 on Saturday afternoon. She tells me she has already met other people, she wants to cover the entire spectrum by age and sex.

I start telling my story, it looks a bit like what I said yesterday in front of the cameras but we talk and we talk. Carole is very attentive, asks well-targeted questions, there is really a feeling between us.

After four hours of conversation and several lemon juices, we keep up with each other and continue on and on.

- *Damn it is 6pm, I must go back to see my family.*

We had talked for 4 hours and did not see the time pass. I walk to the entrance of her building, she really wants to continue the conversation to the end.

Wow, I feel emptied, I stripped naked in front of a stranger but I think it was worth it. Carole is very interested in my profile, she will talk to her editor on Monday, she seems to gloat ...

My last Parisian night is held in a good restaurant with my godson Lucas and his girlfriend. He is a young film director and lives in Paris, that's where things move. I tell him my adventures, so many exceptional things happened in just 2 days.

It is time to return to Hanoi and back to work Monday morning when I arrived at the airport ...

Dad, you're so beautiful

CHAPTER 24

SEPTEMBER 9, 2018, I am in my hotel room with a magnificent view of Tokyo Bay. Tomorrow we have directors' meeting and then we will go fishing in this same bay. Having nothing else to do, I decided to spend the weekend here, lots of shopping opportunities and lots of places to visit.

I get a call from Yoshi, a huge typhoon hit Osaka and the damages at the plant are significant, the meeting is postponed to Tuesday in Osaka. The airport is closed, I will take the train, the famous Shinkansen.

Mike arrives this Monday in Tokyo, he could not change his plane ticket to Osaka. We meet at the restaurant to eat sushi and other sashimi, a treat! In the afternoon, I receive an email from Elise announcing that the show will spend this afternoon on France2 at 2:00pm! They said that the broadcast would be in six to eight weeks, not two weeks! Fortunately, I have not known before, no time to dwell on it.

From my room, I test the VPN connection to view France2 live, the show will be at 9:00pm Japan time.

I go around in my room, how do I present? What I will look like? And my voice, how was it? Have I told nonsense? ...

The opening sequences start, close-up on my face as well as on the other guests, a few key phrases as introduction, Faustine starts.

I see first of all that I am well seated and dressed as it should, my posture is feminine, everything starts well. For half an hour, I listen and watch myself tell my life. Damn, I'm not bad and all I say has sense. Faustina tells me I'm beautiful ... amazing ... Victorine adds a layer, I only cry watching all these images.

End credits, Faustine Bollaert embraces us... what a relief, I'm happy and proud of me ... YES! The first comments arrive by email and on my phone, only messages of support and admiration ...

What recognition for Céline, she exists only for a few months and hundreds of thousands of people look at her. I exist, I am there, I live, I am happy ... Christophe with his permanent anger, his dissatisfaction, his asocial character no longer exists!

In the following days, hundreds of messages arrive from all sides, my parents congratulate me, many cried while looking at me, so many touching messages!

Just back in Hanoi, I get an email from a reporter from VnExpress, the first news website in Vietnam, 90 million connections a week! She has read the article in the Vietnam News and would like to write an article for her website with a video. Both will be in Vietnamese and English.

Why not, I would really like to change things in Vietnam. The government considers that there are 200,000 transgender people in Vietnam but there is not the slightest structure. Most buy injectable hormones on the black market from Thailand. My hormone treatment, I did it entirely with existing drugs from any pharmacy but nobody is informed and almost no doctors know what to prescribe.

Vietnam is the first country in Southeast Asia to have passed a law in favor of transgender people but the road is still long ... The reporter, Huong, will come from Saigon and spend the day with me. She is small and looks very masculine, she certainly did not choose this subject by chance. She begins by filming me at home, my dressing room, my makeup, I take a coffee, I work on a pastel painting ... I play my own role, we redid shots ... Once she had everything she wanted, we go to the factory to continue reporting. Same topo, staging's and interviews of my colleagues, in Vietnamese this time.

She then asks me dozens of questions and I insist heavily on the message that I want to convey:

All drugs for hormonal replacement therapy are available in Vietnam, do not spend your money on products that you have no control and which cost you a fortune.

I have already told my story, it is now the others that must be helped. The article and the video should appear within a fortnight, we'll see.

Like last year, I will participate in the Nuremberg show on the 6th and 7th of October. I'll be back a few days earlier to enjoy moments with my daughter, my parents, my friends. I will combine that visit with the first shooting day for TF1

They have approved my profile, I work hard with Carole to prepare the different scenes and all the topics that will need to be addressed. Shooting will be done in three stages: first in France in Colmar, Vietnam and then Thailand, eight full days of shooting are planned, I cannot imagine at all what that represents. I particularly appreciate that four-hands writing, we really prepare this together.

Arrival in Frankfurt, I rent a BMW M6, a monster of 640 horses can exceed 300 km/h, I have a clear idea of its use during filming.

October 1, 2018, Colmar train station, Carole and the cameraman arrive at 8:30am, a long day awaits us.

The cameraman is called Arnaud, very nice at first sight, Carole had only praise for him. He immediately installs the microphone and receiver hidden in my pant, I'll have to keep it for the day.

We head to Horbourg-Wihr on the outskirts of Colmar to start filming with my sister Stéphanie. Florist by trade, I helped to finance her shop, she is really an artist in her field.

Stephanie had known for a long time the pain that had been eating me, we had spent three weeks together as part of a medical spa treatment in Amnéville.

Carole and Stéphanie worked together for this scene so that my attitude is more spontaneous. Arrived on the spot, Arnaud realizes one of my old dream which returned to me regularly. A big sports car that roars, the door opens, a leg with stockings and heel pumps comes out ... the class ... and very cliché too, I know. Only that sequence takes thirty minutes, I have to do it again and again, it promises.

I finally enter the store and kiss my sister, it does not suit Arnaud, we start again, once, twice, five times ... each time we redo the kisses while trying to be as natural as possible. Of course, under no circumstances should you look at the camera.

We talk about things and others then Carole asks Stephanie about my transition, how she lived it, if I'm different now. Pleasant to hear what she thinks of me, I do not know without this shoot.

My other sister Bénédicte refused to testify as well as my parents, which I understand. Bénédicte has a lot of trouble accepting the media around my story, she was the only one to have said nothing after my broadcast on France2. I respect her, she has already done so much for me, I cannot blame her.

We return to downtown Colmar for lunch, the time passes so quickly and the program of the rest of the day is very busy. After a meal in an Alsatian restaurant, we leave in the valley of Guebwiller, very close to my home and consequently of Jeannette, we have rendezvous at the fishing pond where I spent so many mornings, days and even nights. I had asked Michel if he agreed to testify, he was hesitating but he could not refuse me that.

Arnaud installs him the microphone then we start with the reunion, different shots around the lake and Carole questions about me. Arnaud goes to the other side of the pond to film us from a distance.

- *Camera man is totally crazy, he runs in all directions!*

It is true that it feels like he is fueling with Red Bull, an electric battery but he knows his job, incredible precision and efficiency. He's coming back to us ...

- *In fact, even if I'm far, I hear everything you say, the mikes are open ...*

Oops, we did not think microphones remained connected. When I was in the bathroom, he also heard everything!!! I'll have to be vigilant for the rest of the shoot.

When we return to Colmar, we make a stop in the vineyard to shoot me at the wheel of my super car. Arnaud settles on the side of the road, I make several round trips, too funny to see all the cars slow down and flash the headlights thinking it was a radar.

I walk in the old town of Colmar, I go up and down the street several times, Arnaud filming me sometimes before me, sometimes behind. Circulate as a woman in this city that has seen Christophe grow, passers-by wonder who I am, some recognize me for having seen me on France2, quite exhilarating situation, a beautiful revenge on life. On the other hand, a big mistake on my part: stiletto heels in streets that are all paved, but what an idiot I do.

We meet Stephanie for a shopping trip between sisters. We walk, Carole takes care to keep passers-by from the field of the camera, all eyes are of course placed on us.

We enter one of my favorite shops “Malice Bean”, I'm a regular customer, vendors know that I live in Vietnam and often ask me how I live there.

I ask the manager, Valérie, if she accepts that a team of TF1 shoot in the store. She did not hesitate and we start our shopping and fitting. Arnaud does not enter the cabin, thankfully!

We arrive at the moment of paying our purchases, Carole asks Sylvie if she can ask her some questions:

- *What does it make you to serve a transgender person?*

Sylvie is visibly caught off guard

- *Nothing special, well, we see that the size is different ...*

I obviously see she is annoyed and I am really angry with Carole, the answer was in the question, I really do not agree with her way of proceeding and let her know. A few months later, I saw Valérie, she did not know that I had benefited from a sexual reassignment, it is Carole who taught her. In the meantime, she has watched the film Danish Girl and read a lot of articles about it, she is really charming and very kind.

We finish the evening with a sauerkraut at my sister Stephanie home. My two nieces, Louise and Daphné, agreed to testify, I was not aware. So that Carole and Arnaud can enjoy the sauerkraut, we do the filming during the aperitif. I discover the testimony of my two nieces, how they lived through my transition, I am impressed by their maturity and the way they talk about it.

The day ends after five hours of shooting which will give five minutes to editing, only waste! I'm really at the end, nervously and physically exhausted, it's far more tiring than I thought.

Tomorrow, Arnaud will make some shootings of the city then they will leave towards Paris, the appointment is fixed in fifteen days, on September 15th in Hanoi.

I greet them at Noibai airport in Hanoi, the temperatures are very different than in France, it is still 35° and light clothing is required. They will stay to my home, the Palace, which will save much time. On the other hand, the production of TF1 is very watchful on every penny spent, free accommodation suits them well.

For 4 days, we will shoot at the factory, at home, in the city, at the beautician, nightclub ... Some moments are very strong, it's the first time I'm overwhelmed by my emotions, I cry, Carole cries, Arnaud films, I do not see his eyes. In some scenes, I'm in a nightie, I'm really not comfortable with this big body carcass. In another sequence, I'm in a swimsuit ... Ouch! It is possible to change the facial features and some other parts of the body but the frame will always remain the same as will the size of the hands and feet, you must learn to live with.

I am organizing a big party at home with my colleagues and friends, we are 36, some are interviewed, Arnaud is filming all the way, such a beautiful evening.

Thursday night, we leave for Bangkok, the city of my rebirth. We will meet my surgeon who will make gynecologic examination, I dread it! not the examination but the fact of being filmed during that check-up.

I arrange for Carole to contact Erika, an American who will get sex reassignment surgery in two days, she agreed that the camera follows during this important stage of her life.

We arrive at the clinic, I find Boun who has not changed, always equal to himself. We wait more than an hour for Dr. Sutin to arrive, we take advantage of that time to get to know Erika. She is of androgynous appearance, neutral clothing, no makeup and a relatively serious voice. We are all a bit surprised, we were expecting a more feminine person. Looking back, the day before the operation, I was a man, nothing allowed to perceive my femininity, it is quite odious for me to think about it.

Come the time of the visit, we prepare the scenario with the doctor, he makes sure by 3 times that I agree to film. I am sitting on the gynecological chair almost naked, the camera is behind me, I have no idea what it is filming, I present myself naked in the true sense of the word. Dr. Sutin is very much a pedagogue, he explains in detail what he does, what he controls and gives his diagnosis. Follow-up is an important step in a sex change, and I thought it should be part of the story.

The next day, we finish filming on the river Chaopraya which cross Bangkok, Carole asks me the last questions.

Something strong settled between Carole and me, a complicity, a real friendship. I will have a right to look at the narrative of the report, I trust her, she understood the message I wanted to convey. An adventure ends, a page turns. After six days of incredible intensity, the void! I was well prepared, it is easy to sink into a kind of mini depression when it happens.

Thank you Carole, thank you Arnaud, I look forward to the broadcast.

EPILOGUE

FOR 53 YEARS, I WAS PART OF A HALF OF THE HUMANITY, TODAY I AM PART OF THE OTHER.

I am the happiest woman in the world, not a single second I regret my choice. In my journey, I have experienced no reluctance from anyone, I am aware of being extremely privileged. This transition, I built it over the years, I am convinced that there is no chance. From the day one accepts oneself, appreciates this new image, one becomes invincible.

Thanks to my daughter, my parents, my sisters, Annie, my friends, my colleagues, my therapists, you have all been very supportive and tremendous comfort. A special thanks to Jack Davis for his great support for the English translation.

It is thanks to you that I can assume so easily as a woman, life is so beautiful!

"The fear of dying is nothing beside that of not living."

Dad, you're so beautiful

REFERENCES

TV & videos :

France2 : ça commence aujourd'hui
TF1 : grand reportage
LCI
Vietnam News
VnExpress
Au Féminin
Oh my mag
L'alsace

Newspapers and magazins :

Le Parisien
Femme Actuelle
France Dimanche
Huffingtonpost
Le petit journal
L'Alsace
Les dernières nouvelles d'Alsace
Le républicain lorrain
Est républicain
Vosges matin
Psychologie magazine
Boursorama
Google news

Dad, you're so beautiful

Yahoo news
MSN

Radios :

Vivre FM
Radio campus

Made in the USA
Monee, IL
07 December 2019